Shelley Niro
Seeing Through Memory

On the Series

The Canadian Artist Monograph Series (CAMS) consists of books that focus on presenting the work of Canadian artists. Each volume in this series explores the practice of a single artist, actively participating in the arts and culture of Canada, through critical texts, interviews and copious images.

Series Editors
Miriam Jordan-Haladyn & Julian Jason Haladyn

Shelley Niro
Seeing Through Memory

MADELINE LENNON

CAMS
Blue Medium Press, 2014

Copyright © 2014 by Madeline Lennon
Image copyright © by Shelley Niro
All rights reserved

Edited by Julian Jason Haladyn and Miriam Jordan-Haladyn
Copyediting by Ron Benner and Jamelie Hassan
Images courtesy of Shelley Niro [except where indicated]
Design by Julian Jason Haladyn

Second Edition

ISBN: 978-1-988101-04-0
Published by Blue Medium Press
London, Ontario, Canada
www.bluempress.ca

Contents

Acknowledgments vii
List of Figures viii

First Nations Culture Re-Imagined in the Art of Shelley Niro   1

    I. Meditations on Identity   6
    II. History and the Meaning of Presence   28
    III. Re-envisioning Sky Woman   37
    IV. Great Peace and the Message of Peacemaker   57
    V. Decoding Memory   70

Conversation with Shelley Niro   79

Bibliography   143

Acknowledgments

Shelley Niro has been generous, thoughtful and great fun to work with on this project. Her approach to her artistic production, and to life in general, is inspirational and I have learned from her more than I can fully express here.

Julian Haladyn and Miriam Jordan made it possible for me to undertake this study. My thanks to them for the many enlightening discussions, and the careful editing and suggestions that assisted me and enriched the text. The technical advice of Nanda Dimitrov was invaluable.

-M.L.

Shelley Niro would like to thank her husband Celestino for his kindness, thoughtfulness and much appreciated patience. And to acknowledge and thank Madeline Lennon for her thoughtfulness and care. Her happiness and wisdom made this experience a joyful one. Without Madeline this book would never have been made.

-S.N.

List of Figures

1. *Haudenosaunee Senses*, 2001	3
2. *Kissed By Lightning*, 2009	4
3. *Waitress*, 1986	8
4. *Mohawks in Beehives* and *Queen Bees* from the series *Mohawks in Beehives*, 1991	11
5. *In Her Lifetime*, 1991	12
6. *The Rebel*, 1987	15
7. *The Iroquois is a Highly Developed Matriarchal Society* from the series *Mohawks in Beehives*, 1991	16
8. *Standing on Guard for Thee* from the series *Mohawks in Beehives*, 1991	19
9. *Bagging It* from the series *M: Stories of Women*, 2011	20
10. *Red Heels Hard*, 1991	21
11. *Portrait of the Artist Sitting with a Killer and Surrounded by French Curves* from the series *Mohawks in Beehives*, 1991	22

12. *500 Year Itch* 25
     from the series *This Land is Mime Land*, 1992

13. *It Starts with a Whisper*, 1993 28

14. *It Starts with a Whisper*, 1993 30

15. *It Starts with a Whisper*, 1993 33

16. *It Starts with a Whisper*, 1993 34

17. *The Moon, Me, and the Celestial Tree*, 2010 35

18. *Flying Woman Series*, 1994 39

19. *Flying Woman Series*, 1994 40

20. *Flying Woman Series*, 1994 41

21. *Sky Woman Series: Preparing for the Fall* 43
     and *Losing My Stuff*, 2002

22. *Sky Woman Series: Dreaming* and *Loving it*, 2002 44

23. *Beginnings* 47
     from the series *M: Stories of Women*, 2011

24. *Routes* 49
     from the series *M: Stories of Women*, 2011

25. *Blanket* 50
     from the series *M: Stories of Women*, 2011

26. *The Shirt*, 2003 53

27. *Abnormally Aboriginal*, 2013 54

28. *Parallel Worlds of Women and Warriors*, 2010 58-9

29. *The Essential Sensuality of Ceremony*, 2002   62

30. *The Essential Sensuality of Ceremony*, 2002   63

31. *Kissed by Lightning*, 2009   64

32. *Kissed by Lightning*, 2009   67

33. *Kissed by Lightning*, 2009   68

34. *Seeing With My Memory*, 2000   71

35. *Basket Series*, 2012   72

36. *Suite: INDIAN*, 2005   83

37. *Warning*   86
   from the series *This Land is Mime Land*, 1992

38. *Always A Gentleman*   89
   from the series *This Land is Mime Land*, 1992

39. *Robert's Paintings*, 2011   90

40. *Suite: INDIAN*, 2005   95

41. *Passage*, 1996-97   96

42. *Honey Moccasin*, 1998   101

43. *Kissed by Lightning*, 2009   111

44. *The Shirt*, 2003   112

45. *Suite: INDIAN*, 2005   115

46. *Treaties*   118-19
   from the series *Borders-TREATIES*, 2008

47. *Unbury My Heart*, 2000-2001   121

48. *Passing Through*, 1993   124

49. *Ancestor*   127
   from the series *M: Stories of Women*, 2011

50. *Memories of Flight*   128
   from the series *M: Stories of Women*, 2011

51. *Finding Her Helpers*   129
   from the series *M: Stories of Women*, 2011

52. *Land of Opportunity*   130
   from the series *M: Stories of Women*, 2011

53. *The Essential Sensuality of Ceremony*, 2002   132

54. *Ghosts, Girls and Grandmas*, 2004   135

55. *Ghosts, Girls and Grandmas*, 2004   136

56. *TREE*, 2007   138

57. *Requiem for an 1812 Forest*, 2012   139

First Nations Culture Re-Imagined in the Art of Shelley Niro

> *In a contemporary context, I like to parallel the myth with my life and the lives of people around me.*
> — Shelley Niro[1]

With these words, Shelley Niro captures the essence of her artistic production. She examines the history of her people communicated through their stories, using her personal experience to understand and visualize the knowledge contained in Iroquois legends. In this process memory is central. However, the very idea of memory is complex: it relates to the individual and the collective; it is linked to material production and to ritual; and it is enlivened through narrative. For example, a central vision in Niro's work is enabled by her father's stories about the original home of the Mohawks, in the mountains of what is now New York State.[2] The beauty of the Adirondacks and of the Mohawk River valley was palpable for her father, and his descriptions and tales of the region are a significant part of his children's memories. Yet it seems that her father's reality was a cultural memory, not one he had actually experienced because he had not visited that region. Thus, one of the many ways Niro knew her father was as a storyteller, a bearer of the oral tradition that brings the past into contact with the present so that the reality of a people continues to unfold. When she finally visited the place herself, seeing the vistas of the valleys and the river brought her father's stories and her own mental images to life.

This personal connection between story and reality is an important factor in Niro's ability to activate the stories or legends of the Iroquois through artistic representation. Recognizing the layered meanings of her works requires that we remain open to the many ways she interweaves the significance of history and legend with the actuality of contemporary life and current events. These connections consistently appear in the details of her work. In the lithograph *Haudenosaunee Senses* (2001), images of DNA strands are presented in a way that resemble strings of wampum beads – white and purple beads carved from shells that were used to record agreements, among other things.[3] Whether the wampum is a framing device or represented as part of a healing ceremony in Niro's work, it references the long history of beading as a traditional form of 'writing' or language used by First Nations peoples, primarily women, for centuries. Wampum also plays a key role in the legend of Peacemaker, who is central in the history of the Haudenosaunee or People of the Longhouse because he brought the Great Law of Peace to fruition in the twelfth century. His various actions in uniting warring tribes come to life in her representations of natives today.

The interweaving of history/legend and contemporary life also functions more broadly in Niro's practice. We see this in the story of her film *Kissed By Lightning* (2009). Niro takes the plight of a young widow, Mavis, living on the reserve, an artist painting the stories about Peacemaker told by her late husband as she prepares for an exhibition at a New York City art gallery. Her paintings, interactions with others on the reserve and the appearances of ancestors at telling moments in her story connect past and present in often moving ways. This film

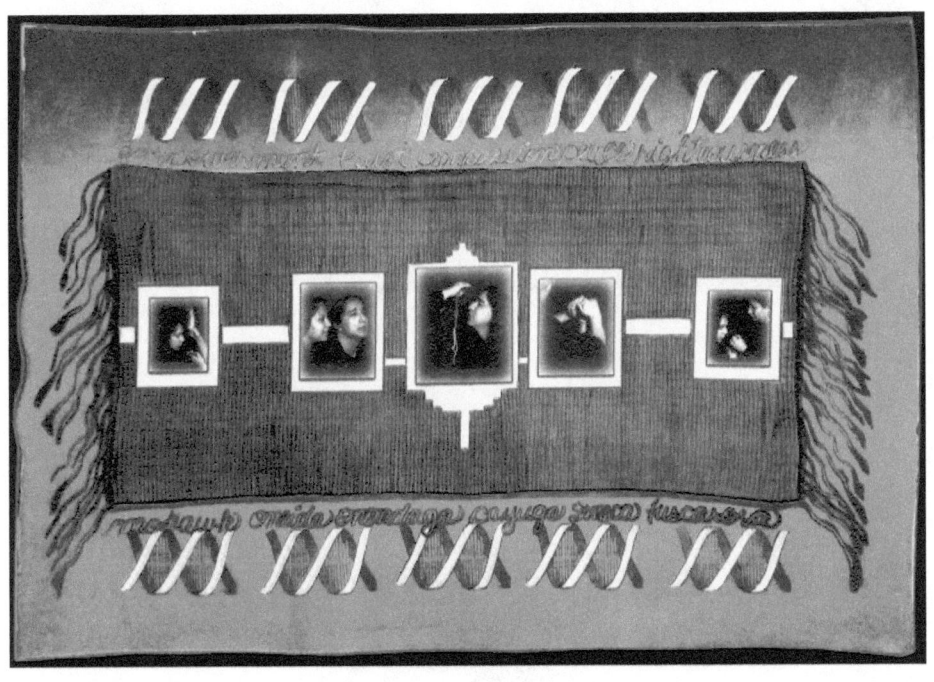

1. *Haudenosaunee Senses*
   2001
   lithograph
   102 x 60.9 cm

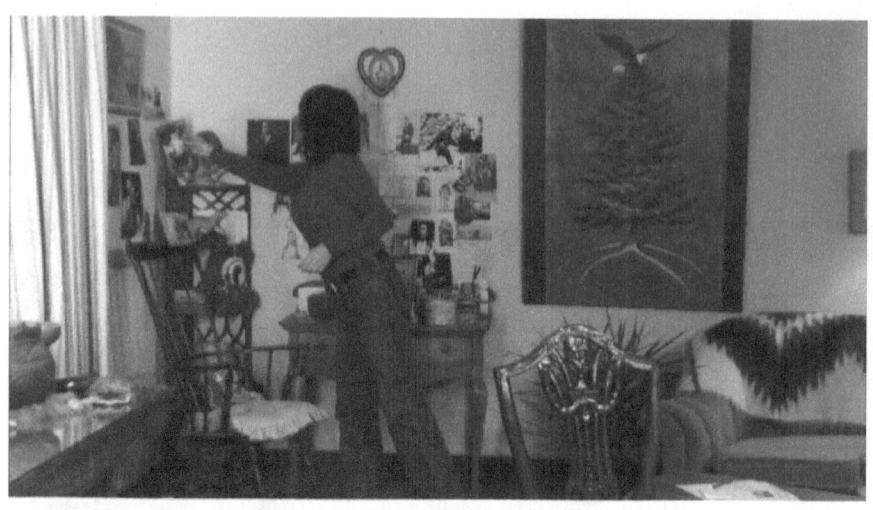

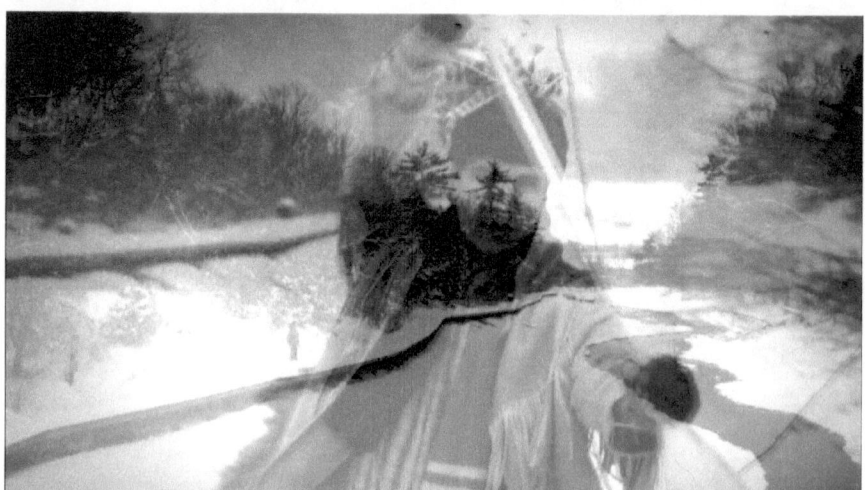

2. *Kissed by Lightning* [film stills]
   2009
   HD video, colour
   90 minutes

and the story of Peacemaker are discussed in more detail later in the current text, but I wish to note here Niro's use of the artist's journey driving from the reserve to New York City when she is shaken by apparently accidental detours. These unexpected encounters connect her with people from other cultures who value her as a Mohawk and with her husband's own living ancestor – his grandmother who Mavis meets for the first time. In Grandmother Josephine's home, faced with visible memories of his family and their lives (photos, news clippings, objects), she recognizes the magnitude of what she had missed through ignorance and avoidance. With each experience of this journey Mavis confronts her own fears and losses, gradually accepting the invaluable harmony offered by her own heritage.

Throughout *Kissed By Lightning* the beauty and power of nature is captured in stunning images, communicating the basic theme of the harmony of all creation. The land is the source of strength, the place where connections to their history and people come alive. The land, as well as the legends connected with it, forms the strong ground on which Niro bases her work. To this ground, she adds cultural and personal histories – of family, of community, of ritual and of creative production – to form a rich resource that she mines in her explorations of what it means today to be First Nations, Indian, Native, Aboriginal. This I take to be the overarching theme of her artistic practice.

I. Meditations on Identity

The breadth of Niro's production, encompassing almost every type of traditional and contemporary artistic medium from painting to beading to film, addresses topics and issues that reflect the two main cultural perspectives she inhabits. Primary and central, of course, is her Iroquois status. Niro is a member of the Turtle Clan, Bay of Quinte Mohawk; she grew up on the Six Nations Grand River Reserve in Ontario, Canada, with her parents George Oliver Doxtater and June Chiquita Doxtater, along with four siblings. On the other hand, Niro was born in Niagara Falls, New York. She earned a Fine Arts Honors degree at the Ontario College of Art in Toronto and a Masters of Fine Arts degree at The University of Western Ontario in London; currently she lives with her husband in Brantford, Ontario (with daughter and granddaughter nearby) and travels widely through North America and Europe. She is a woman of her time, an artist whose work is based on her Native heritage, while it also reflects her experience and understanding of non-Native, Western culture.

As a child encouraged by her father who recognized her artistic abilities, raised in a creative atmosphere where everyone was engaged in making things, she was especially taken with drawing. She responded to the heroes of Western art represented in museums – such as Leonardo da Vinci and Michelangelo – and worked hard to hone her drawing skills, a process that she later linked closely to painting. At the same time, the historic and contemporary images she saw of her own people varied from those negative, stereotypical representations of mass media, television and Hollywood films, to the romanticized images of such photographers as Edward S. Curtis who in the 19th century considered the Indians a dying race. However, none of these images reflected what she saw around her, what she knew of the lives and personalities of her family, friends and community to be. Her frustrations with this disconnect and with the daily reality of racism propelled her to produce the powerful painting *Waitress* (1986).

    The artist represents herself as a waitress who, gazing down, is serving a glass of wine to a seated customer. But the wine is spilling and the woman looks up at her with a shocked, angry look. In the background a couple – Brian Mulroney, the Canadian Prime Minister at the time, and his wife Mila Mulroney – are dancing and laughing, completely wrapped up in themselves. They do not see the flaming faces that form a wall of glowing spirits behind them, nor the Celestial Tree floor decoration. The painting vibrates with strong colours and a dense surface. The images here refer to the artist's experiences around this time: being pointedly ignored and treated badly by a sales woman; seeing television reports of Brian Mulroney meeting with Native leaders from the First Nations who were speaking with him about their concerns and worthwhile initiatives, while he smirked and looked bored – in effect, treating these leaders disrespectfully. The waitress figure is a strong individual who seems not at all upset by her action of spilling the wine, on the contrary; she appears quite thoughtful and controlled. At the same time, her blouse and hair reflect and seem activated by the fiery faces that form an aura around her head. We can

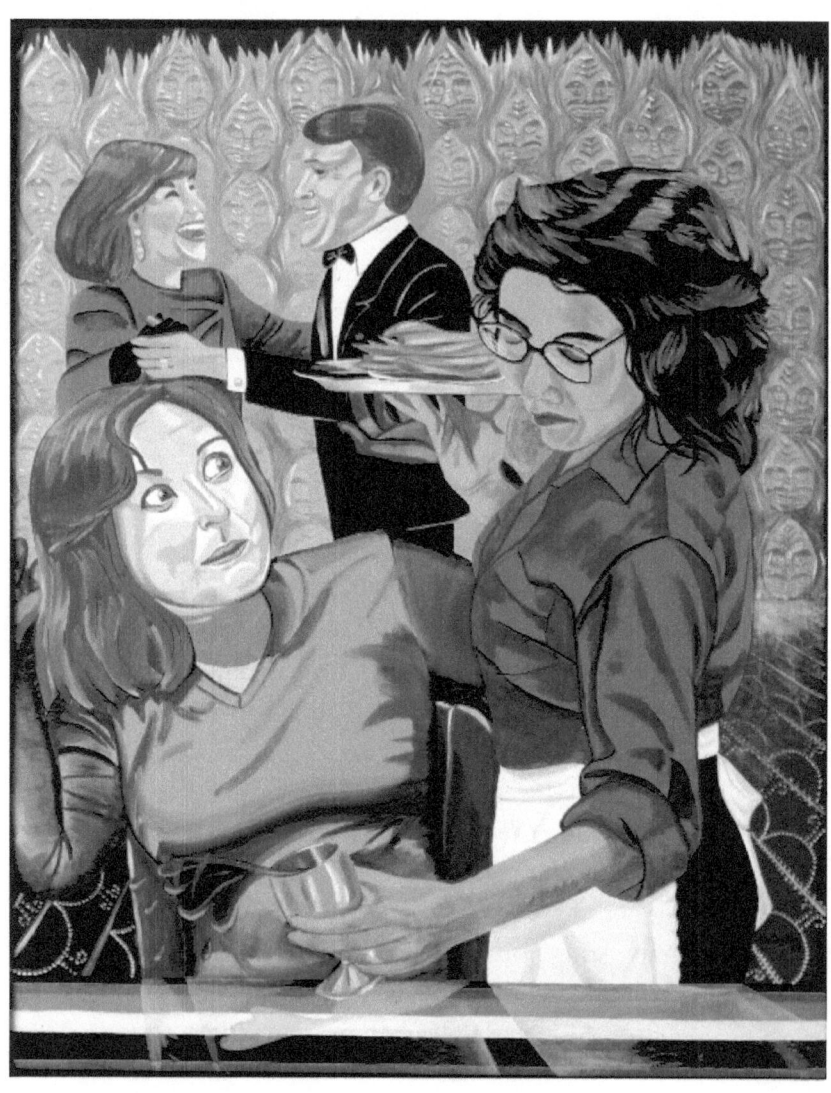

3. *Waitress*
   1986
   oil on canvas
   91.4 x 121.9 cm

read this painting as an expression of a simmering anger in response to her reality and also of the strength and support that she finds in the spirits of her traditions and culture.

In this early painting there are several threads that Niro developed through her career. The first is Niro's response to the depressing situation of the First Nations people in North America: she would not wallow in depression. Instead, she worked out how to use and move away from the anger that is palpable in *Waitress*. This was not an easy shift, given constant exposure to television reports of terrible confrontations between government forces and First Nations people in Quebec and elsewhere who were demanding that their land rights and other treaty rights be represented and upheld. Local newspaper editorials consistently denigrated First Nations people, who became the focal point for much animosity – with many shop employees being rude to the point of racism. Niro recognized the toll this was taking on her, her family and community. In response, she turned to art and the notion of personal responsibility for one's life. Her strength of character shines here, as she enlisted her sisters to work with her to enact the joy in their lives. Documenting this joyful fun resulted in one of her most popular works, *Mohawks in Beehives* (1991). This series of fourteen photographs could be subtitled: *Mohawks who are regular women having a good time*. Any viewing audience can connect with their antics. While her work is not always this light-hearted, she consistently uses a thoughtful, personal approach to unpack and comment on the situation of First Nations peoples. The result is never dogmatic. It is quietly persuasive – achieved at times through her approach to the subject and other times through her choice of materials (such as colourful beading or touches of bright colours added to black and white photographs).

The second development concerns her discovery of photography, a medium that became a key mode of expression in her artistic practice. Niro discovered its potential in a course on printmaking that included a section of instruction on traditional photography. As it turned out, her work with printmaking led her to experiment fruitfully with photography.[4] Though painting was still important for her, the immediacy of photography and its open, malleable possibilities meshed with her growing desire to represent her reality. I believe photography spoke especially to her tendency to narrate – to tell a story. In the painting *Waitress*, there are a number of actions underway: spilling wine, people dancing, flaming faces; connected narratives are represented. Photography can do this even more effectively (and later, film). And what better medium to choose to counteract the romanticizing historical and current negative photographic representation of Indians?

Consider *In Her Lifetime* (1991), a series of six hand coloured black and white photographs that are headshots of a native woman whose thoughtful expressions reflect the message of the text written on the photos. The whole reads like a personal narrative:

In her younger years she was quite carefree, laughing, singing, dancing.../
she would look out to the horizon and let her thoughts drift out with
the never-ending tide./

As maturity set in she became depressed over the fact that soap operas
had no ending, country music reminded her of soggy cornflakes/
she could never find the matching sock to the one she held in her hand...and/

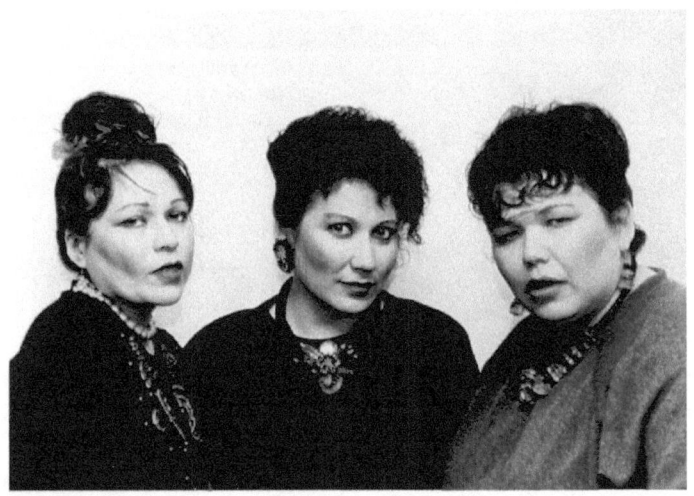

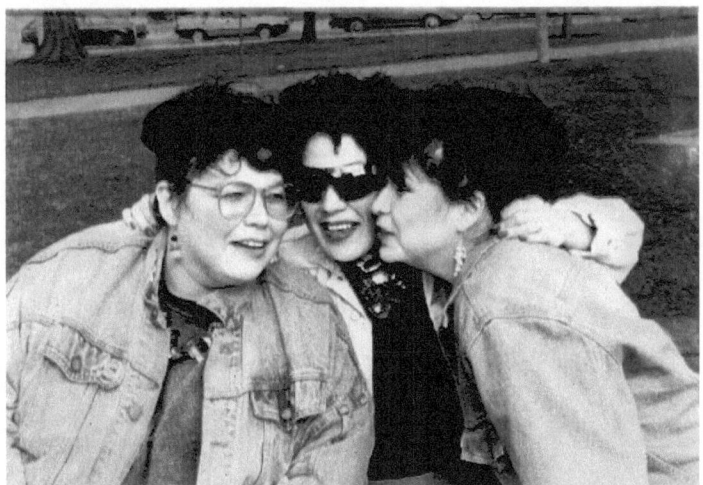

4. *Mohawks in Beehives, Queen Bees*
   from the series *Mohawks in Beehives*
   1991
   14 hand-tinted black and white photographs
   dimensions variable

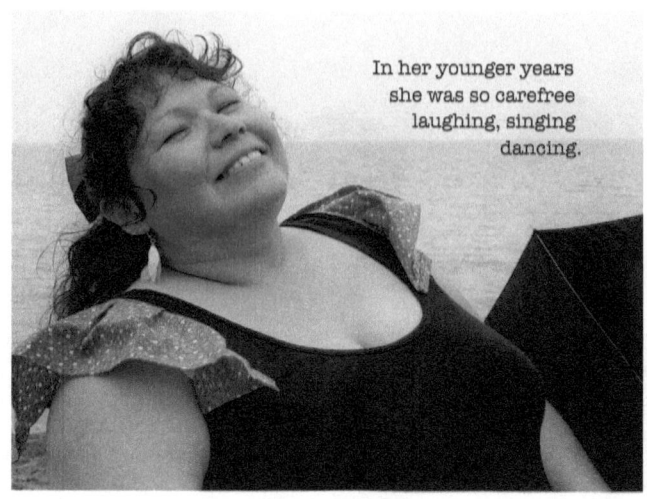

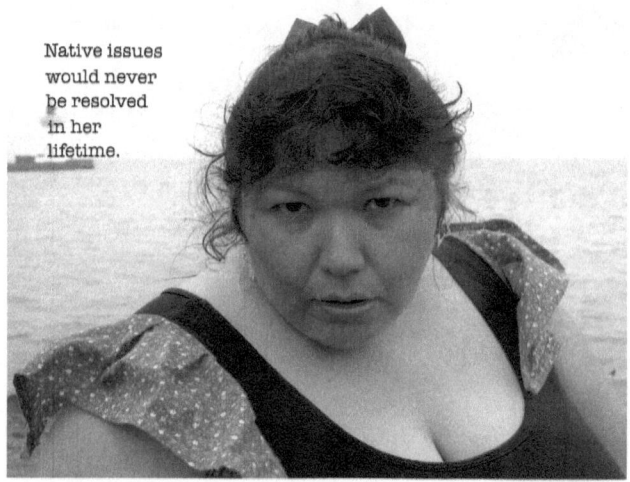

5. *In Her Lifetime* [#1 and #3]
   1991
   series of 6 hand-tinted black and white photographs with text
   [mounted horizontally in a single mat]
   25 x 20 cm [each]

Native issues would never be resolved in her lifetime./

*She would give herself a shake and realize Christmas was six months away,
the kids would be out of school soon and Friday was just a day away.*

This text is a perfect example of the connections that surface in Niro's work as she struggles to make sense of the contradictions and conflicts in her personal life and in the larger world around her. As with *In Her Lifetime*, several photographic series of the same period respond to cultural situations through her personal perspective.

When the series *Mohawks in Beehives* was first exhibited it was recognized as a very different kind of depiction of Native women.[5] The series of hand-tinted black and white photographs show women who are having fun, dressing up and enjoying themselves in town. The titles of the works in this series reflect Niro's sensibility: *Mohawks in Beehives 2, The Iroquois is a Highly Developed Matriarchal Society, Queen Bees, Standing on Guard for Thee, Spring Fever, I Enjoy Being a Mohawk Girl, Mohawk on a Cloud, Portrait of the Artist Sitting with a Killer Surrounded by French Curves*. The implied light-heartedness contrasts with the narrative of the impulse for these photos: the shocking political events of 1990 and 1991, specifically two events that affected Niro profoundly on a personal level. The first is the confrontation between Mohawks and the Canadian army in Oka, Quebec. Natives protested the town's decision to use for a golf course land they considered sacred – this was the immediate cause of the resistance. However, it seems clear that given all that had been lost by First Nations people across Canada, due in large part to the impossibility of counting on Treaty agreements with the Canadian government, it was time to take a stand. Television coverage of the standoff was unrelenting and exacerbated the potential for racism in the media and in society generally. The situation continued for three months through the summer of 1990 and, as Niro pointed out, the "constant hammering of events about [Native] people in the compound left me in a state of depression and confusion."[6] The second is the Gulf War with all the bombings and destruction wreaked by the American armed forces that, four months after Oka, was broadcast all over television. Niro was overwhelmed by the repeating violence.

Her response was to represent her reality: Natives who are feisty, strong and witty. *Mohawks in Beehives* set the tone, picking up on an idea she explored in an earlier photo *The Rebel* (1987) that depicts her mother posing on the trunk of the family car. Her mother and three sisters all seem to enjoy posing and acting out positions of women as pictured within popular cultural entertainment, except allowing their own personalities to shine through. This personal, quirky approach to representing her family in terms familiar to most people (no matter their heritage) is appealing, while at the same time conveying Niro's questions about stereotypes imposed on Natives. We see this in *The Iroquois Is a Highly Developed Matriarchal Society*, a triptych of photographs that show the artist's mother under a hair dryer laughing and playfully hiding her face as she relaxes in the kitchen of her daughter – who is described as the family "hair sculptress."[7] Niro turned the ethnographer's dry formulaic description on its head. What does it mean to live in a matriarchal society? It depends on your mother! In this case, it seems that through her sense of humour and her creativity Mrs. Doxtater was a significant influence on Shelley and her siblings.

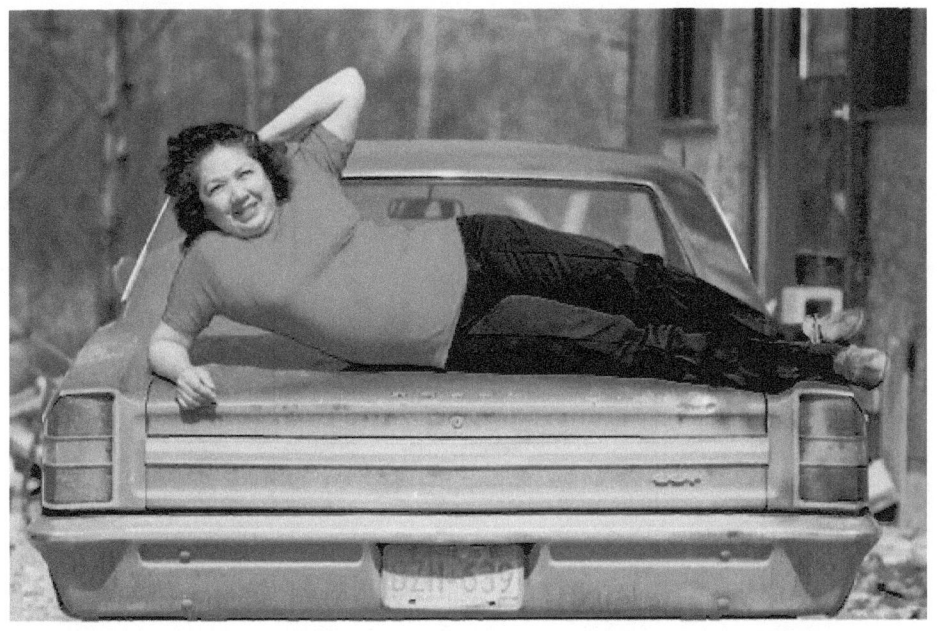

6. *The Rebel*
   1987
   colour photograph
   24 x 16.5 cm

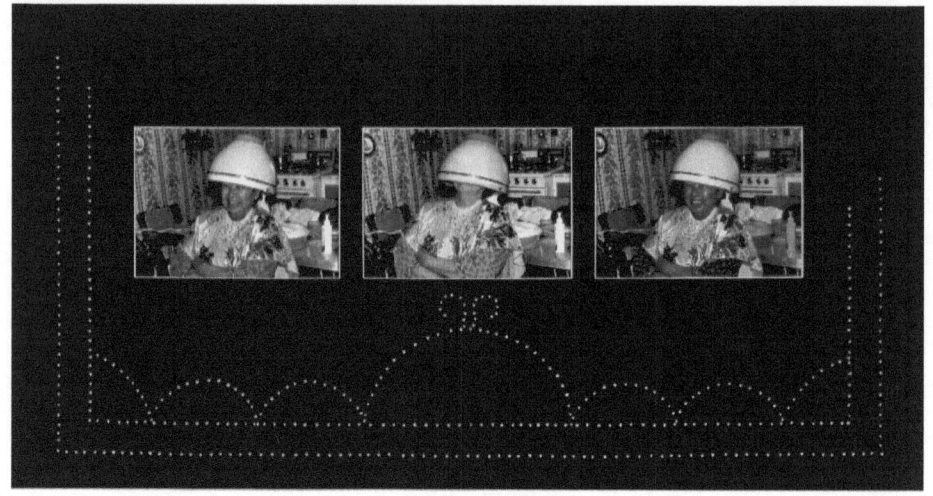

7. *The Iroquois is a Highly Developed Matriarchal Society*
   from the series *Mohawks in Beehives*
   1991
   image courtesy of Linda Grussani, Director and Kevin Gibbs, Art Registrar, Aboriginal Affairs and Northern Development Canada

For Niro the question about a matriarchal society rankled. Painfully aware of the dysfunctional family relationships and the mistreatment and dishonouring of women in Native communities, Niro contemplated the role of women in Iroquois history and how colonization had destroyed the balance in many First Nations families. Originally, Iroquois women had control over their lives and equality with men in their community. While men traveled to trade and hunt, women remained with the Longhouse, tending the crops, caring for the families and organizing food and clothing. Among modern anthropologists, some have interpreted this organization as the subjugation of the women, but this is a misinterpretation and misunderstanding of the organization of this society. Traditionally, Mohawk women were seen as creators who understood the rhythms of nature and were entrusted with much of the organization and decision making of the community. After marriage, the man lived with his wife's family; in this matrilineal society, their children became members of her clan. It was always the women who selected the leaders and who chose representatives to attend meetings with other nations.[8] However, after contact, the European colonial authorities rejected any notion of a significant role for women and acted to undermine women's status by assigning titles and new roles to the men. This degrading of the fine balance in Mohawk life culminated more recently with the infamous residential school system that tore families apart, destroying languages and belief structures. In the face of this history, ethnographic studies of First Nations read like accounts of a lost race.

Niro considers that, despite the fractured lives of some First Nations people (those lives so often highlighted in the media), there are actually more who are like her family. The sense we have of the Doxtater family is conveyed through her representations – closeness, respect, caring, and creativity. Her pictures resonate with a positive, down-to-earth reality. Memories of her parents reflect hard-working, happy people who created a supportive environment for their children despite the poverty on the reserve. She speaks, as well, of her father's service in the armed forces in World War II and his serious attention at commemorative ceremonies that they all attended.

Thus, when Niro took her sisters to the street, choosing as a backdrop the impressive monument to Joseph Brant in the center of Brantford, there are broader reverberations. *Standing on Guard for Thee* is an ironic reference to the Canadian national anthem while highlighting the historically significant Native figure of Brant.[9] At the same time, there are echoes of the reality of her father's life – his war service contrasting with his life on the First Nations Reserve. Where and how exactly do First Nations people and their leaders fit into this history and Canadian society? Niro references the Brant monument more obliquely in other works, such as her use of the sculpted plaques depicting Mohawk warriors decorating the base of the monument – for example, in *Bagging It*, from the series *M: Stories of Women* (2011). These recurring figurative quotes suggest the ways she considers what is left of Mohawk history that is visible, who produces that history and what this means for contemporary representations of First Nations peoples.

Another photo taken at the same time as *Mohawks in Beehives* and used in the series *Red Heels Hard* (1991) gives us the sisters 'kicking up their heels' in front of the same monument. These are not downtrodden, depressed women, nor are they the angry, confrontational people that were pointedly used to fill newspapers and television screens. Niro's response to those popular images was to

First Nations Culture Re-Imagined

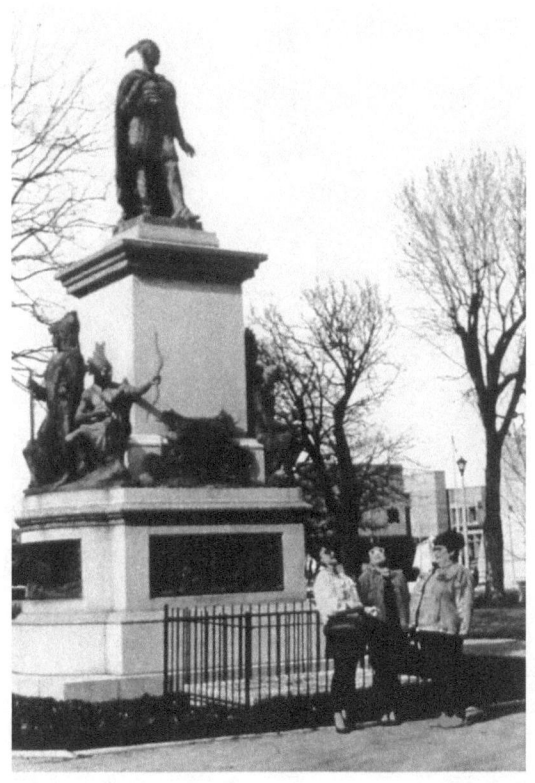

8. *Standing on Guard for Thee*
   from the series *Mohawks in Beehives*
   1991

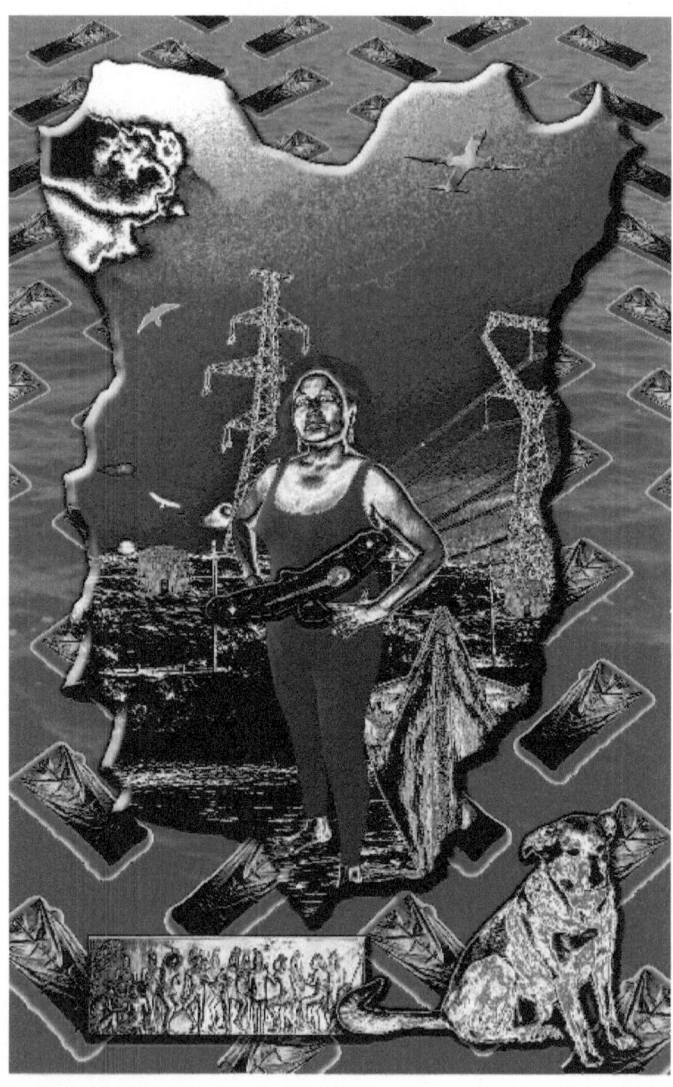

9. *Bagging It*
   from the series *M: Stories of Women*
   2011
   series of digital prints
   101.6 x 152.4 cm

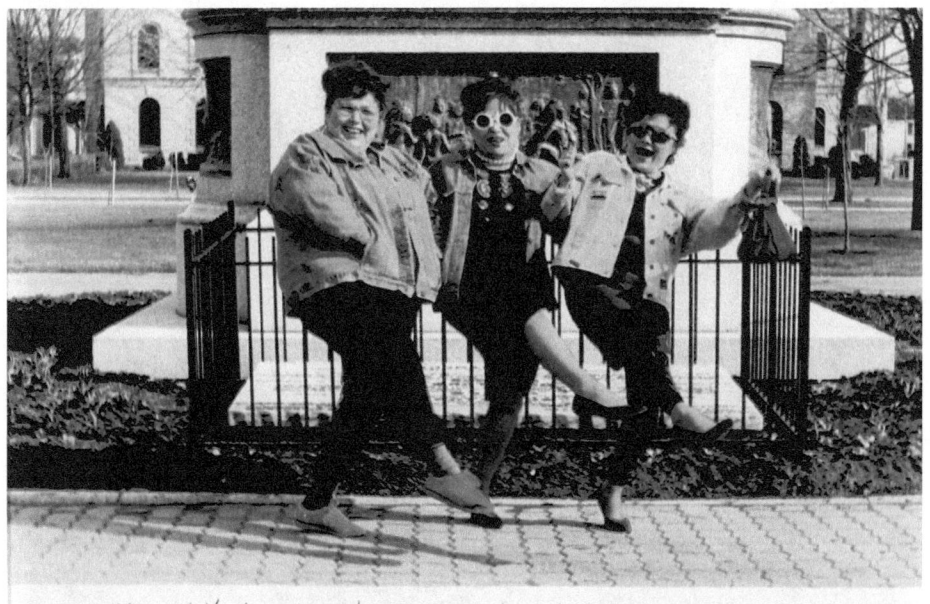

10. *Red Heels Hard* [#5]
    1991
    series of 6 hand-tinted black-and-white photograph
    [mounted horizontally in a single mat]
    26.5 x 21.2 cm [each]
    image courtesy of Linda Grussani, Director and Kevin Gibbs, Art Registrar, Aboriginal Affairs and Northern Development Canada

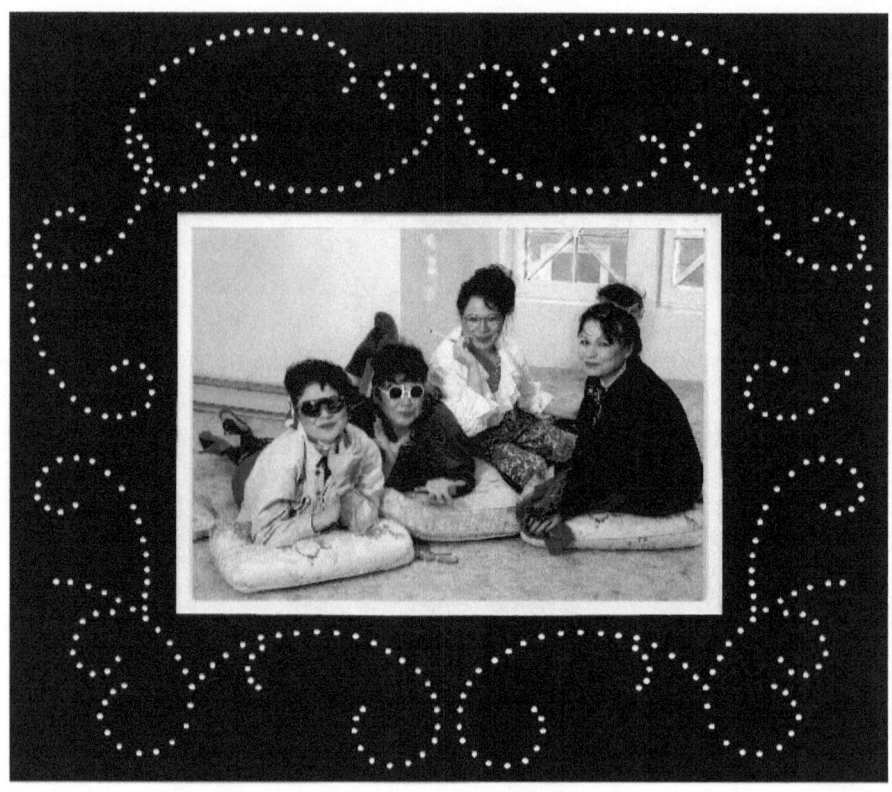

11. *Portrait of the Artist Sitting with a Killer and Surrounded by French Curves*
    from the series *Mohawks in Beehives*
    1991

present another reality emphasizing the humorous and the human. She fashioned appealing images whose message is enhanced through the colour she applied to the black and white photos. In her hands, the potentially grey life of black and white is animated by the flashes of reds, pinks and blues. Her action suggests the ability of people to decide for themselves what and how they want to be, rather than simply accepting the biased media definitions.

Even the frames of *Mohawks in Beehives* are part of the message. Niro drilled small holes in the black mat board, which are arranged in decorative patterns that reflect imagery found in traditional beadwork. Using a dremmel drill, she created swirling designs that are modern versions of the Celestial Tree, which is an important element of traditional decorative beading patterns on clothing, textiles and related objects. The Celestial Tree is an iconic image for the Haudenosaunee and is linked with their legend of the creation of the earth and of humans. The rounded shape of the image locates the founding of the earth on the back of a Great Turtle, while the upward spray references the great tree of Sky World that figures significantly in the tale of origin. While it is an image central to the history and beliefs of the Haudenosaunee people, it may also reference Niro's membership in the Turtle Clan, Bay of Quinte Mohawk.

In *Portrait of the Artist Sitting with a Killer* and *Surrounded by French Curves* the artist depicts herself smoking a cigarette, sitting with her sisters around her, all with bright make-up and smiles. Their enjoyment in acting out is palpable and this sensuous feeling is picked up in the curving designs drilled in the black mat that frames the scene and echoes the lines of their bodies. These framing designs work in tandem with the photographic compositions, reiterating the double context of Native and non-Native cultural histories and experiences.

The second series from this same period is a more self-focused meditation on identity. *This Land is Mime Land* (1992) consists of twelve panels, each with three photographs arranged horizontally (triptych-like) in a mat that, like *Mohawks in Beehives*, is decorated with hand-drilled designs. Each panel reads like a personal meditation on Niro's own identity in the context of family and culture, with titles that are again quite telling: *This Land Is Mime Land, Judge Me Not, 500 Year Itch, Love Me Tender, Survivor, Camouflaged, Santa is a Dene, Final Frontier, Mohawk Worker, Always a Gentleman, North American Welcome, Warning of Snow*.

Moving from left to right in each panel, the first photo depicts Niro in costume; the second, sepia-toned, presents a family member from her own archive of family photos; the third is the current Niro in relaxed garb and different poses. The panel of the work's title has Niro first in white-face, costumed elaborately and posing like a mime; her five-year-old daughter, in the sepia-toned central print, in a sweet, slightly embarrassed pose; and in the final print the artist in her work clothes stands with her back to the camera, hand on hip, looking into darkness. This panel is challenging to interpret but suggests that she considers herself as potentially 'miming' the ideas of Western culture, in contrast to the naturalness of her daughter, and then looks beyond her immediate surroundings to another space, to another possibility for self-definition. The idea of miming as opposed to a 'true' sense of self and self-expression permeates the whole series. At the same time, this series is like a meditation on how we are formed by the different cultures that we experience as we mature, from our family heritage to a variety of influences here encompassing Native and Western cultural expression.

First Nations Culture Re-Imagined

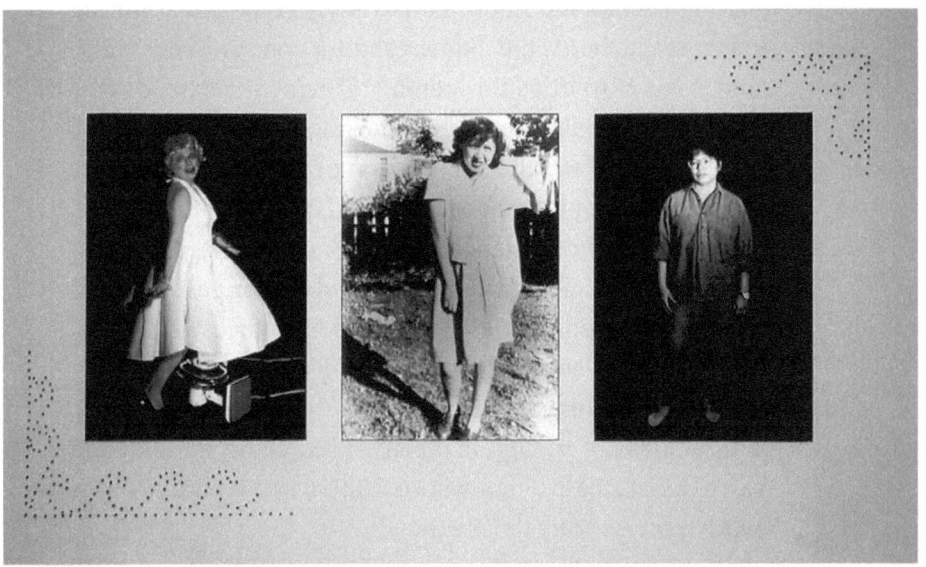

12. *500 Year Itch*
    from the series *This Land is Mime Land*
    1992
    hand-tinted gelatin silver prints in hand-drilled overmat
    94 x 56 cm
    image courtesy of Rachelle Dickenson, National Gallery of Canada, Ottawa
    Photo © National Gallery of Canada/Musée des beaux-arts du Canada

One of the most frequently cited photographs in this series is *500 Year Itch*. A laughing Shelley Niro poses as Marilyn Monroe in a blond wig with the iconic white dress blowing in the breeze – reflecting the famous scene from the 1955 film *The Seven Year Itch*. But she pokes fun at the iconic image with her literal vision, which pictures a small fan set on the floor that is visibly responsible for the breeze as she holds the camera shutter control in her right hand. That Niro titles this panel *500 Year Itch* extends the reach of her meditation to embrace the whole of the period of colonization and the subjugation of the North American Natives. Parallel to her pose as Marilyn is her mother's in the central photo, standing outdoors in an elegant dress with a self-conscious and appealing shoulder gesture. In the final panel on the right, a serious Niro faces and looks directly at us. The contrast of the Hollywood goddess and the lovely June Doxtater speaks to different yet parallel ideas of beauty. Is the artist searching for another way to exist as a woman who is Native and who lives in contemporary Canadian society?

The challenge is to consider the implications of all twelve panels – from Snow White to Elvis, from Santa to the Statue of Liberty. What does it mean to have models that do not reflect your own reality and history? If she is first and foremost a First Nations woman, an Iroquois Bay of Quinte Mohawk of the Turtle Clan, how can she relate to this other dominant culture that in so many ways denies her existence? Her choices are represented in the parallels with her family photos that identify the most truthful reality. There is something unnerving in the juxtapositions. Seeing the simplicity and honesty of the family in the face of the overblown costumed Niro makes one wonder about the ability of individuals to 'hold their own' in the face of such powerful (if at times ridiculous) icons. At the same time, the strangeness of Niro in these roles can help us understand the anxiety that the individual's attempts to 'fit in' can provoke. Referencing the popular Woody Guthrie song *This Land is My Land* reiterates the central issues: whose land is it, really? How can cultural exclusivity be resisted to insist on the validity of Native identity?

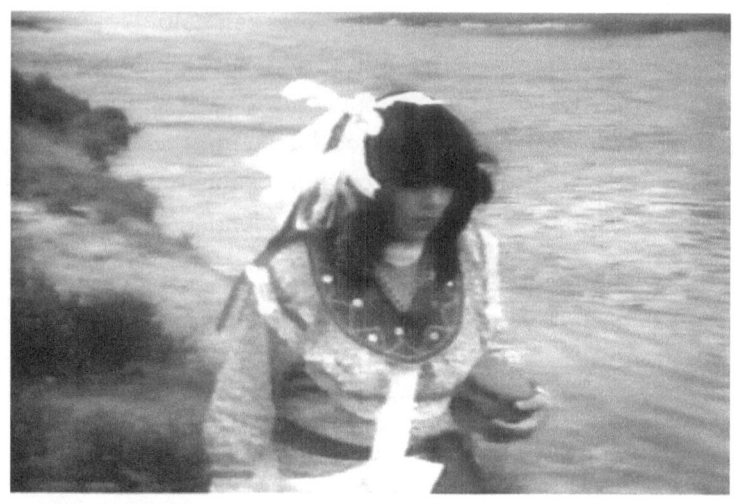

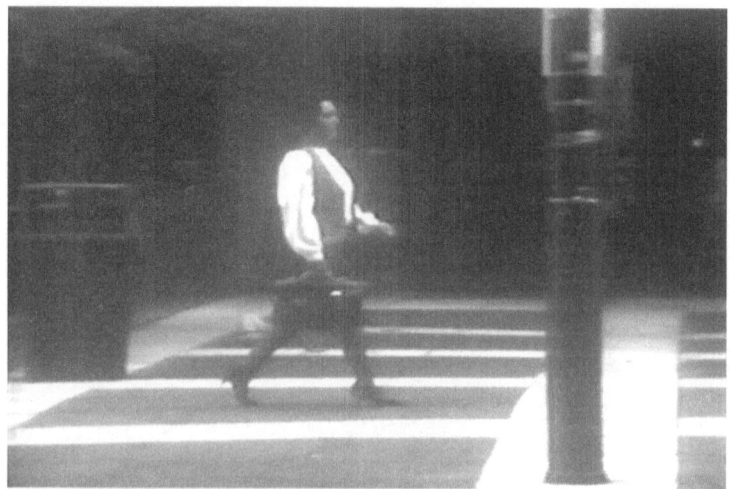

13. *It Starts with a Whisper* [film stills]
    written, directed and produced with Anna Gronau
    1993
    16 mm film
    26 minutes

II. History and the Meaning of Presence

The year 1992 was significant as the 500th anniversary of the arrival of Christopher Columbus on this continent. Many celebrations were planned to commemorate the event, with little or no recognition of the dark underside of this so-called discovery. For Niro, the combined effect of the Oka standoff with all the negative media coverage and the celebratory status of 1492-1992 was the impetus not only for *This Land is Mime Land* but also for her first significant film work, produced and directed with Anna Gronau, *It Starts with a Whisper* (1993).

She responded to these events by examining Native reality through the experience of a young Iroquois woman as she struggles with the oppositions inherent in being part of both Western and First Nations cultures. Shanna Sabbath is the central character, first seen walking along a river, the Grand River on the Six Nations Reserve, wearing traditional beaded clothing. The voices of her Tutelo ancestors speak to her about the history of the First Nations and the disappearance of most of the Tutelo people from the region. She is discouraged by this lack of presence of her history. The scene shifts to the big city, Toronto, where she responds to Western cultural ideals, taking in the urban setting wearing a short skirt and high heels. As Shanna struggles with despair over the difficult life path she faces her three aunts appear and invite her to join them for a New

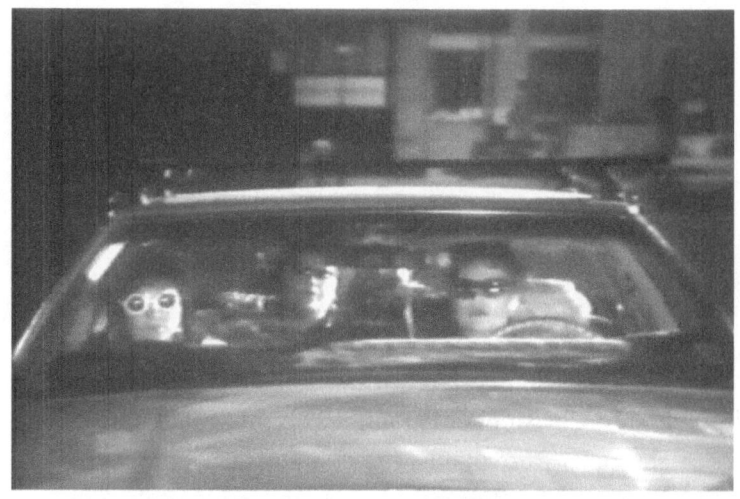

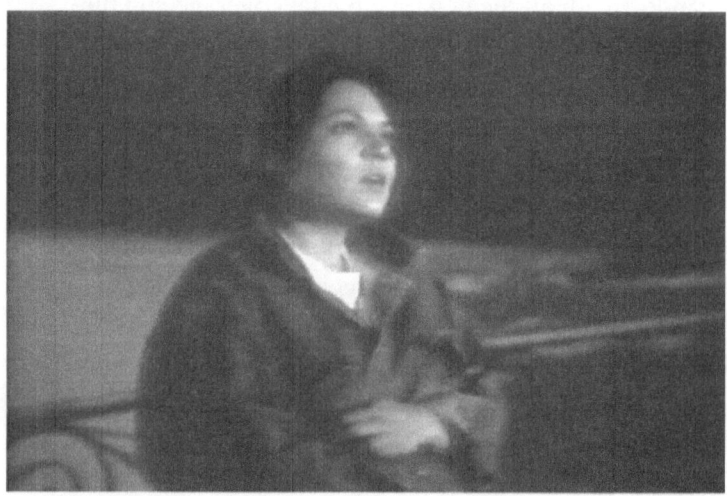

14. *It Starts with a Whisper* [film stills]
    written, directed and produced with Anna Gronau
    1993

Year's holiday in Niagara Falls. These characters, identified as Matriarchal Clowns, feel like extensions of the *Mohawks in Beehives* crew – in fact, they are the same three sisters who cavorted with Niro in the Brantford photo series. It is as though the rhythms and narratives of the photographs in the related series *Mohawks* and *Mime Land* come to life through the moving images of film – Niro's move into this medium representing another significant step in her practice.

Choosing Niagara Falls as the setting for Shanna's transformative experiences is an effective way to draw lively comparisons between the two key value systems being explored. The tackiness of the development around Niagara Falls – overbuilt with souvenir shops, wax and other museums and the brightly lighted, busy tourist attractions in general – contrasts with the natural beauty and majesty of the roaring waterfalls in the traditional lands of the Haudenosaunee.

At first Shanna is annoyed with her aunts who seem to ignore her state of mind. But a conversation she has with the famous Native politician Elijah Harper, who appears to her in a cloud-like vision, helps to reposition her understanding of the past and the present, and leads her to appreciate the strengths of the three women and to see her place beside them. That Elijah Harper agreed to appear in the film as himself is a tribute to Niro, a sign of his trust. He is an iconic figure – the person who in 1990, when he was an elected member of the Manitoba legislature, stopped the voting on a new constitution (on procedural grounds) that led to new negotiations in which his goal was national recognition of Native rights.

In *It Starts with a Whisper* Elijah Harper gives Shanna wise counsel through an understanding of history as it effects the present. His final message to Shanna is to recognize the complexity in contemporary existence but also to feel free to be herself when choosing how to live her life. Significantly, *It Starts with a Whisper* uses messaging layers of voices to communicate historical facts that relate to First Nations as well as to Western people and events. There are a number of examples. Early in the film there is the Thanksgiving address, traditional at the beginning of special events even today. Later Shanna runs to the Falls and hears specific significant dates in her head, among them 1066, 1492, 1924; the dates signify disturbing times for First Nations. At another point she hears the names of the many tribes, including those that were wiped out. It is at this point that Elijah Harper appears to her and they have an exchange about her feelings and his advice to think about these things but to also live her own life. Thus she can embrace her personal value and celebrate the New Year with her aunts as they turn to Native rituals with food, song and drumming.

Counteracting Shanna's depressed state and to cheer her up, the aunts bring humour to this scene through irony, parody and straightforward camp. In their elaborate honeymoon motel room with its heart-shaped bed they joke, dress up and carry on, performing old songs with their own lyrics that speak to their gutsy resistance and independence:

> *I'm surviving, I'm thriving,*
> *I'm doing fine without you.*

And as the New Year arrives at midnight December 31, 1992, the women watch fireworks over the Falls – brilliant lights in the sky that take the shape of the Celestial Tree on the Turtle's back from the Iroquois story of creation.

As noted above, the Celestial Tree appears consistently in Shelley Niro's work, including as a prominent design on the mats of the *Mohawks in Beehives* series and as a key reference in her creative self-portrait

First Nations Culture Re-Imagined

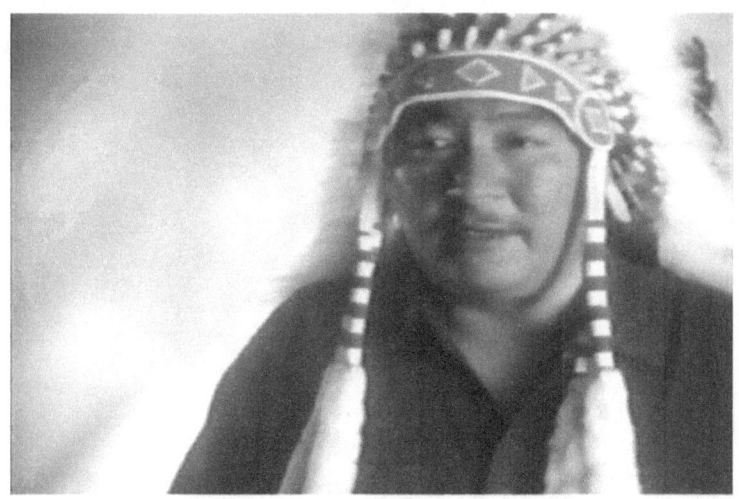

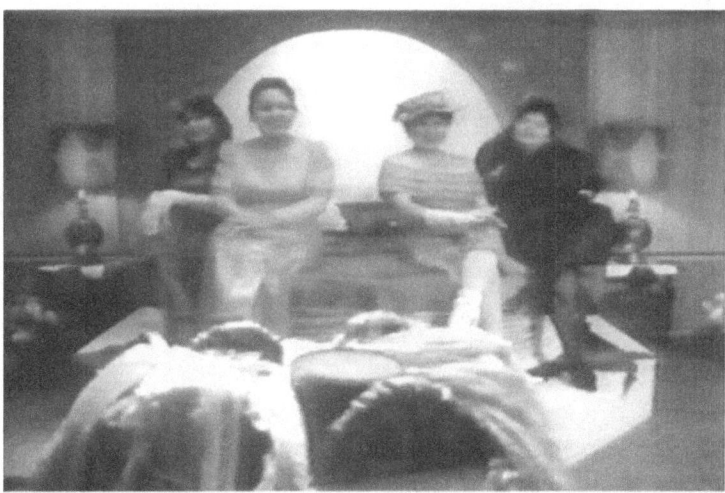

15. *It Starts with a Whisper* [film stills]
    written, directed and produced with Anna Gronau
    1993

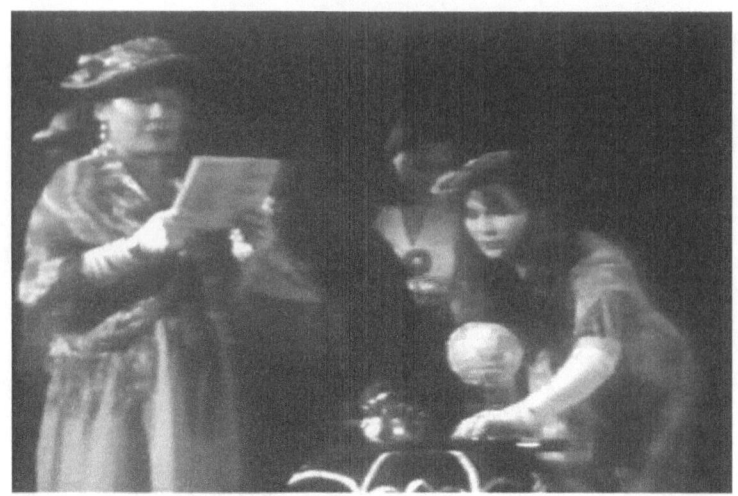

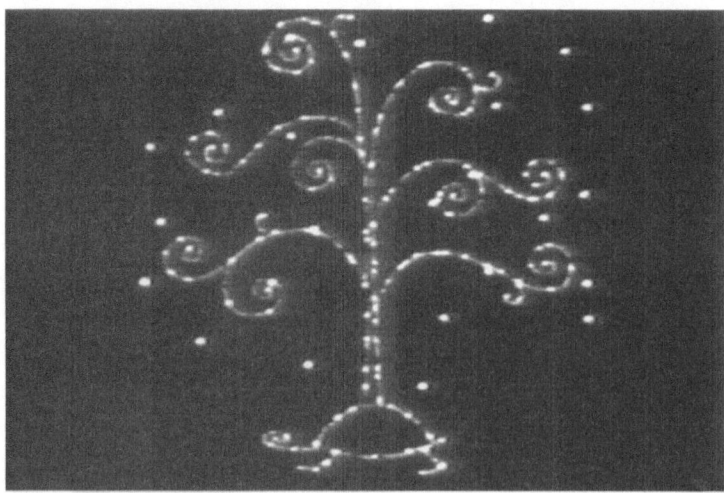

16. *It Starts with a Whisper* [film stills]
    written, directed and produced with Anna Gronau
    1993

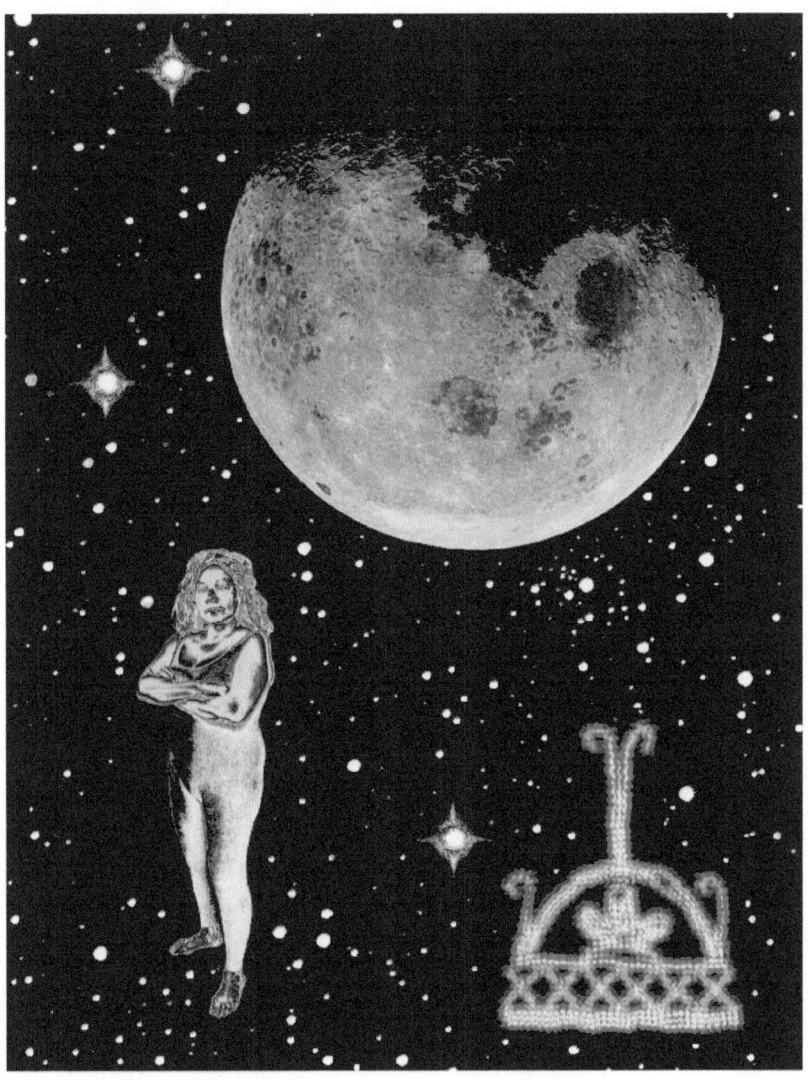

17. *The Moon, Me, and the Celestial Tree*
    2010
    digital print
    152.4 x 101.6 cm

The Moon, Me, and the Celestial Tree (2010). It is one of the most important images in the Iroquois world, expressing the Nation's identity and history. Traditionally it was part of decorative beading and the image in the night sky over Niagara Falls evokes this history of beadwork. Ending the film with this image is a powerful reference that takes the viewer back to the opening imagery of the range of beaded objects, traditional and contemporary, from moccasins to pin cushions. Fire also plays a role here, with flames flickering over the objects.[10] Into these flames the young woman is tossing things that represent what is holding her back. The final image of *It Starts with a Whisper* brings together fire and beadwork in the fireworks imagery, which is a sign of hope in the future – for Shanna and for the Iroquois and First Nations. 500 years of colonization draws to a close; young people have the future to secure their places in a reconfigured world.

Niro's use of film as an artistic medium speaks to her desire to address and bring to life histories that reverberate with meaning in contemporary experiences. We can see how the narrative quality of her photographic works, with their multiple panels and written texts, presage her move to film. Writing the screen play is an opportunity for her to work out her ideas and concerns that focus mainly on the challenges First Nations women have in their lives, in their personal goals and relationships, whether they live on or off reserve. Working mainly with First Nations actors and musicians, she has developed a respected body of filmic work that is recognized internationally, appreciated by Native and non-Native audiences alike. She uses the very 'presentness' and accessibility of this medium to entwine other forms of visual culture such as dance and painting in every story reflecting the richness of the contemporary Native scene.

III. Re-envisioning Sky Woman

For Niro, the histories of her people are central guides to the present. Given her concerns about Native women's lives, it is not surprising that the story of Sky Woman is a central reference in Niro's work. There are slightly differing versions of this complex story that explains the origin of the earth. The main components have it that a special woman, predestined to found the earth, lived in the land of Sky – Niro identifies this as the night sky constellation of the Pleiades. She married an Ancient (a special elder) and became pregnant. Her story is linked with sacred Sky Tree or Great Tree of Life that grew in the centre of this world, holding it together and supplying food for the people. According to one version of this narrative, the Ancient was ill and asked his wife to go to the Tree of Life for water, which was forbidden. Nonetheless, she went to the Tree to gather water and found there a hole in Sky World with a view of the waters far below. Gazing down on these dark waters Sky Woman slipped over the edge, tried to grasp a branch to save herself but fell through the hole with torn plants in her hands, including strawberry and tobacco. (The plants she carried are sometimes described as the "Three Sisters" and could include corn, beans, squash, strawberry or tobacco – all plants that became important resources for Iroquois farming communities).[11]

Sky Woman fell toward the watery world below. Creatures who live in this realm observed her falling toward them and decided to help her. Birds flew up to guide her descent; other animals such as the beaver dove deep into the water and gathered earth for her landing. The Great Turtle offered his back for the earth and on this she landed, dropping the seeds from her hands into the fresh earth. On this earth Sky Woman gave birth to a daughter. Thus the Iroquoian story of Creation posits the central role of woman as founder, giving birth to the people of earth through her daughter, establishing the Mohawk lineage. Her actions reflect the importance of the female role in every aspect of life, including agriculture (woman took responsibility for farming in their communities). Her story is central to the Haudenosaunee belief system and provides vibrant visual references such as the Great Turtle Earth and the Great Tree, as well as the 'falling' woman. She is described as "the First Woman, the First Mother, and the First Grandmother on Earth" and "Our Grandmother Moon, Sky Woman's last face."[12] Niro turned to this figure when she wanted to depict "something expressing freedom, no boundaries,"[13] bringing Sky Woman up-to-date in a number of works.

The earliest of these is the *Flying Woman Series* (1994), ten photo collages depicting a contemporary Mohawk woman in flight. In the summer of 1994, Niro had a residency at Syracuse University and decided to work intuitively with the idea of woman floating free in the modern world. She developed photographs that she had taken of her friend Teresa Marshall and created images by flipping the negatives, duplicating and cutting them up, pasting and drawing around them creating mirror images (these were pre-Photoshop days) resulting in a kaleidoscopic effect. Among the situations she created,

First Nations Culture Re-Imagined

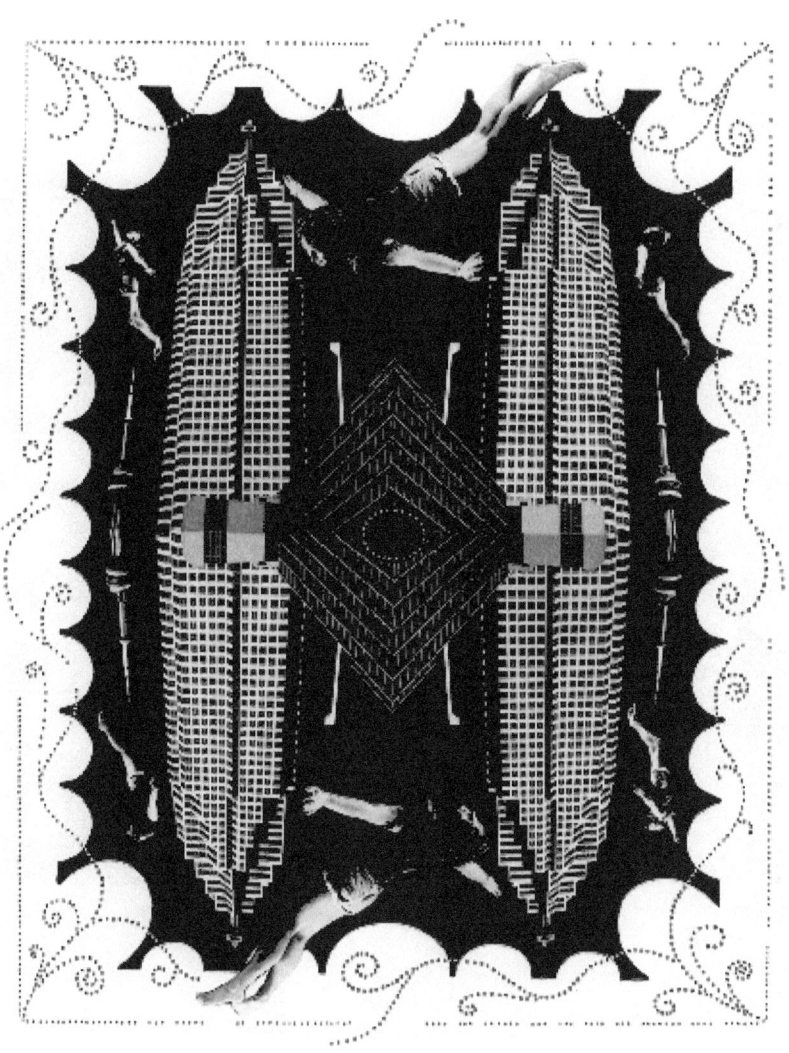

18. *Flying Woman Series* [#3]
    1994
    series of 10 black and white photo collages
    dimensions variable

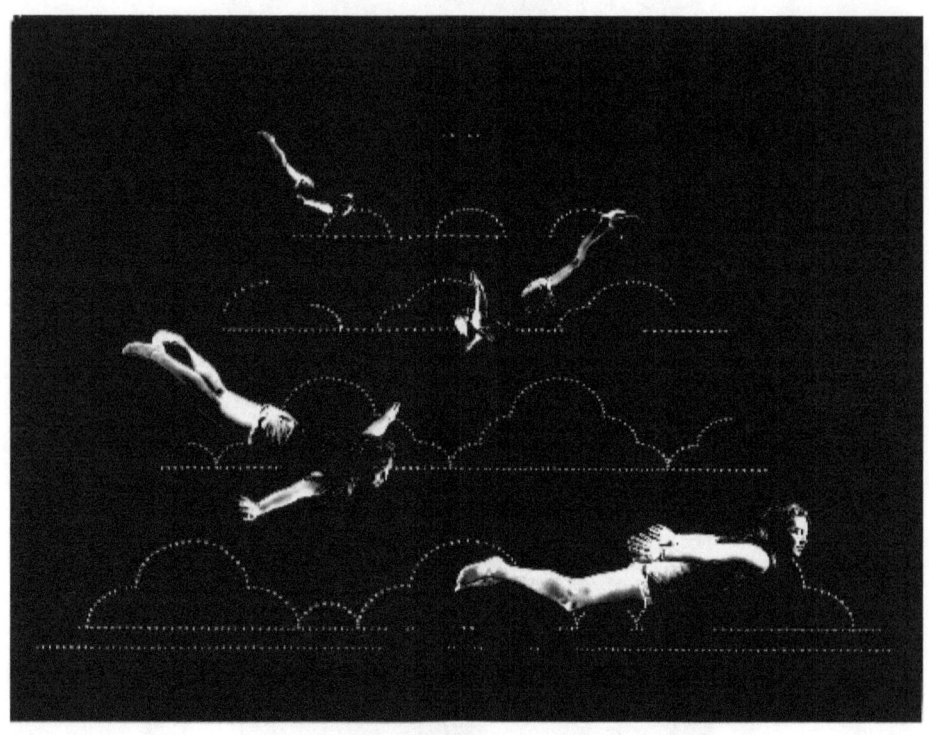

19. *Flying Woman Series* [#8]
    1994

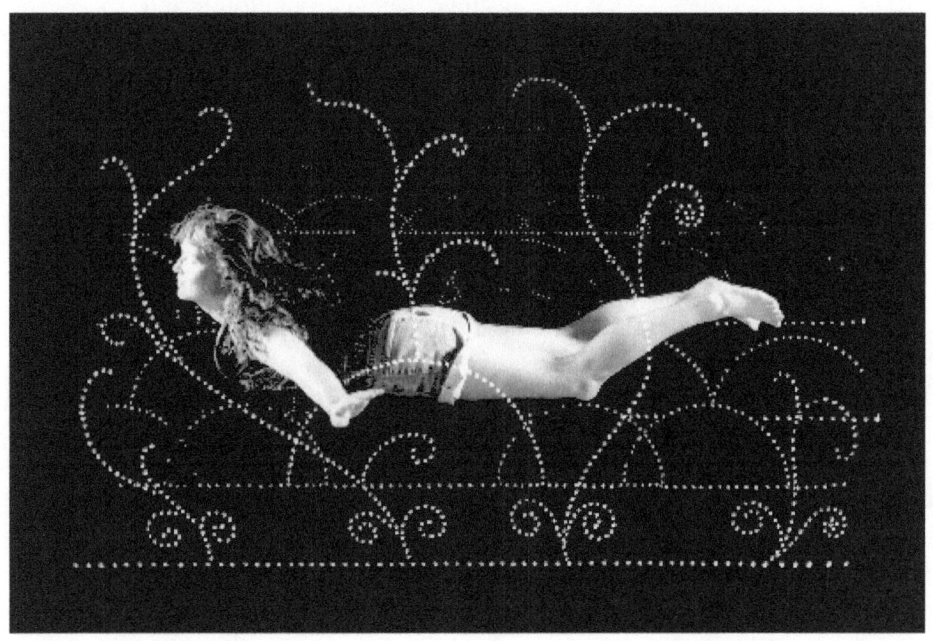

20. *Flying Woman Series* [#10]
    1994

her flying woman encounters Earth Man in the form of Toronto skyscrapers and Elders who are Hoodoo sandstone structures in Alberta. Niro also brings in references to traditions of beading and the Celestial Tree in one photo-collage where repeating images of the floating woman become ever smaller as she descends past clouds and the Celestial Tree that are all suggested by light dots, referencing beading designs. The young woman seems to be enjoying her trip, and she is everywhere. A sense of freedom and quiet satisfaction permeates these images; it is as though Sky Woman observes the contemporary world and all that is possible as she 'falls/flies' from the past into the present. The design of each collage has a rhythm of its own, activating the space and guiding our eyes.

The photo-collages have an experimental quality – both in form and content. Imagining what is possible, Niro plays with the possibilities of photography (eventually she would find 'Photoshop' and move to another level of production). Through this series she effectively reconstructs traditional Sky Woman into someone who belongs in our world.

The sense of Sky Woman's isolation is evident in a series of four colourful pastel drawings, *Sky Woman Series* (2002), where Niro envisions the legend in contemporary terms. She captures first her attempt to keep from falling, grabbing at the plants, with her hair, blanket and purse/medicine bag flying (*Preparing for the Fall*), and then her losses as she drops: her blanket and sunglasses fly off and her moccasins disappear as she tumbles (*Losing My Stuff*). Time passes in this fall and gradually she looks to her future – to the child she is expecting and the energy she will need for

First Nations Culture Re-Imagined

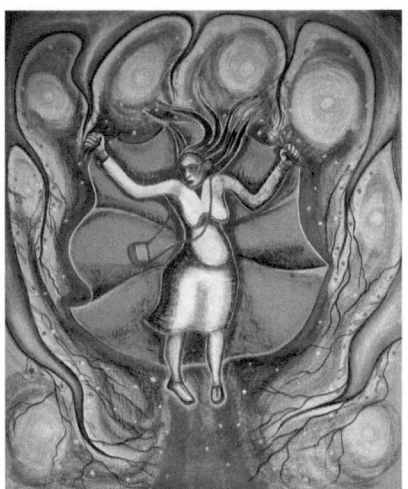

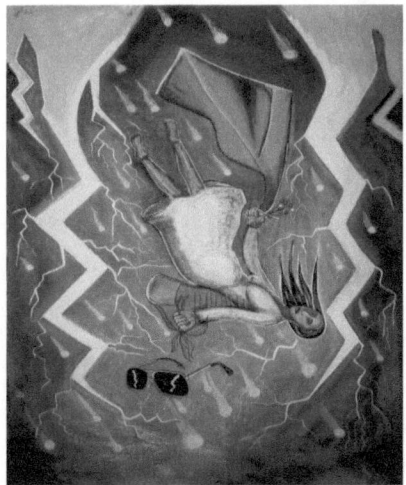

21. *Sky Woman Series: Preparing for the Fall, Losing My Stuff*
    2002
    series of 4 oil and chalk pastels
    127 x 160 cm [each]

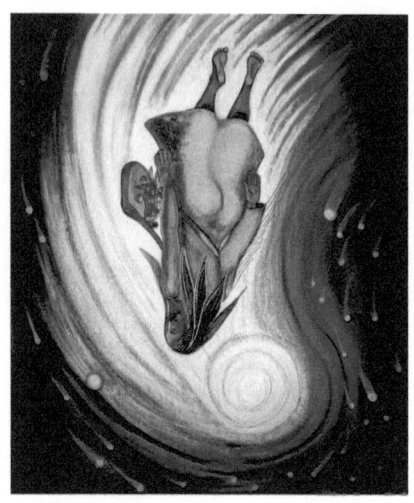

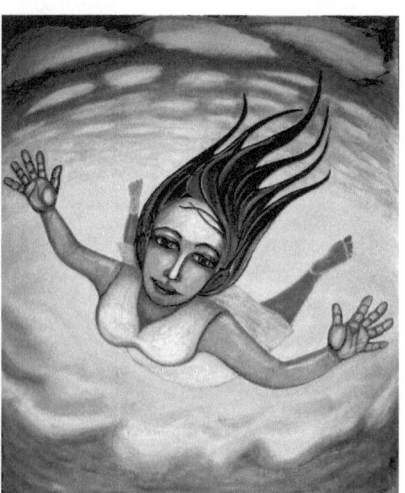

22. *Sky Woman Series: Dreaming, Loving it*
    2002

her new life (*Dreaming*). Finally, Sky Woman faces her situation directly, finds her inner strength and joy, looking forward to relationships with the creatures of this new world (*Loving It*). The first pastel drawing establishes Sky Woman as a powerful and modern figure. She is upright, clutching the plants, looking down towards the unknown with some concern. Her red blanket forms a parachute-like background for her, effectively separating her from the world she leaves behind with its roots, plants and glowing lights. As she falls, her surroundings gradually empty until she appears to float freely in the clouds.

While this series refers very directly to the Iroquois account of creation, more oblique references appear in many of Niro's works. In *Moon and Me and the Celestial Tree*, for example, the artist portrays herself in the heavens contemplating the large, powerful moon and the stars where she is in a free state and can imagine anything. Like Sky Woman, she sees no limits to her future as she approaches the Great Turtle Earth, here represented by the iconic Celestial Tree in the lower right – an image that we find often in her work, a schematic rendering of Turtle/Earth topped by the Great Tree. The powerful moon hovering above the artist is a favoured image. The Moon Ceremony celebrated by the Haudenosaunee in early June and early October "honors Grandmother Moon, women, and all female life that perpetuates the Great Circle of Life."[14] Niro depicts herself as a small heavenly figure, standing strong, arms crossed and firmly planted feet, with the majestic Moon and Celestial Tree, empowered by her people's history and the centrality of Woman as Creator.

Niro is well aware that the role of women in traditional

Iroquoian society was a powerful one. Agriculture was the major economy and this was the female realm – women grew the food, made the important decisions for family and clan; leadership was established through matrilineal succession. The men were the hunters and protectors. Niro notes that European colonizers did not accept this social structure and in fact went out of their way to undermine this traditional way of life.

M: Stories of Women (2011) is a series of digital prints that takes up this issue by focusing on contemporary situations. One panel in the series is a self-portrait: *Bagging It*. Here Niro stands, hands on hips, in a landscape filled with hydroelectric poles; the sky is filled with comets and a large flying bird. This scene is framed in a shape of an animal skin, referencing woman's traditional role in preparing these skins. The bright red background that seems to extend around and behind the 'skin' is punctuated by repeated rectangular shapes that are body bags – Niro's visual commentary on the horrible recent 'mistake' made by the Canadian government when a Northern community was sent body bags instead of flu vaccine.[15] In this context, the brilliant red vibrates with her anger over such inhumane behaviour. Her beloved dog Brandy stands in the lower right corner, balanced on the left by the image of a sculpted plaque from the monument to Joseph Brant that is part of the narrative of his life. These figures from the past and present are her solace, part of who she is. This may be the most devastating image of the series despite the comfort of her history and her pet.

All but one of the prints in the series *M: Stories of Women* feature a variety of animal skin shapes to highlight the central figure. The exception is *Beginnings*. The expressive face in profile of Niro's daughter Naoga is set against the watery earth. This Sky Woman has touched

First Nations Culture Re-Imagined

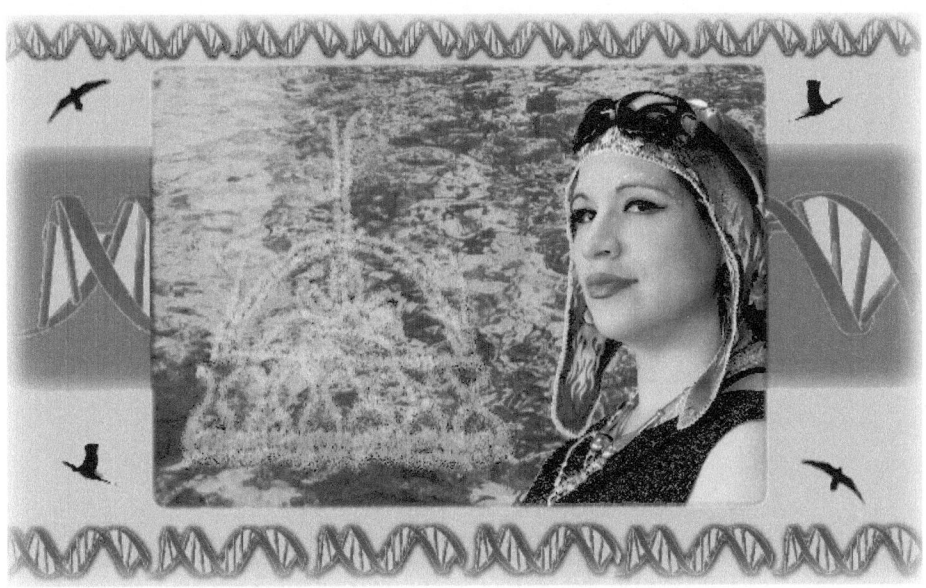

23. *Beginnings*
    from the series *M: Stories of Women*
    2011
    digital print
    152.4 x 101.6 cm

down, wearing an old-fashioned aviator-type hat with earflaps (made by the artist), her sunglasses perched on top. The Celestial Tree icon seems to hover before her as a traditional beaded image – we have seen this in the closing fireworks of *It Starts with a Whisper* and drilled in the mats of *Mohawks in Beehives*. It is a potent reference for Niro, calling up Sky Woman's experience and the Turtle in the Creation story because life springs from it once she lands on the earth covering its great shell back. In the margins of the rectangular frame of this image are the birds in flight who guided Sky Woman to earth and references to wampum in twisted DNA sequences – along the top and bottom, centered at right and left. This single image captures the essence of the Sky Woman creation story.

All the women who figure in *M: Stories of Women* are strong individuals who translate the traditional roles of women for today's world. The artist envisions them as counters to the pervasive media images that discredit Native women as non-contributors. The panel *Routes/Routs* presents Jacquie Carpenter from James Bay standing defiantly with the waters of the Bay behind her. The image filling the red frame area is an aerial view of Toronto. At the bottom, hands present a canoe and beaded work evoking history: early explorers were dependent on the Cree people as guides. The image titled *Blanket* evokes the famous Hudson's Bay blanket with its coloured stripes – but here the background four horizontal stripes are the traditional colours representing the four directions (North-South-East-West). Cree Winnipeg artist Jackie Traverse stares dolefully through the skin-shaped cut-out frame, as though meditating on the devastating history of the traders' treatment of the Natives – gifts of blankets infected with small pox that decimated the Native population; using Native knowledge and experience to take over Native

First Nations Culture Re-Imagined

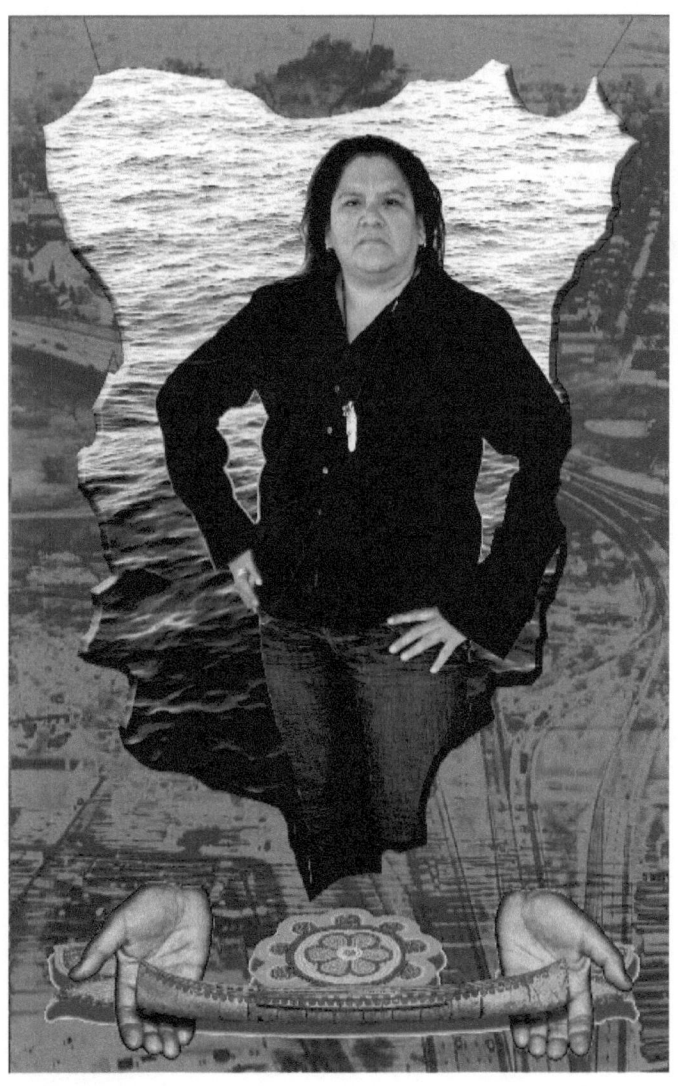

24. *Routes*
    from the series *M: Stories of Women*
    2011
    digital print
    101.6 x 152.4 cm

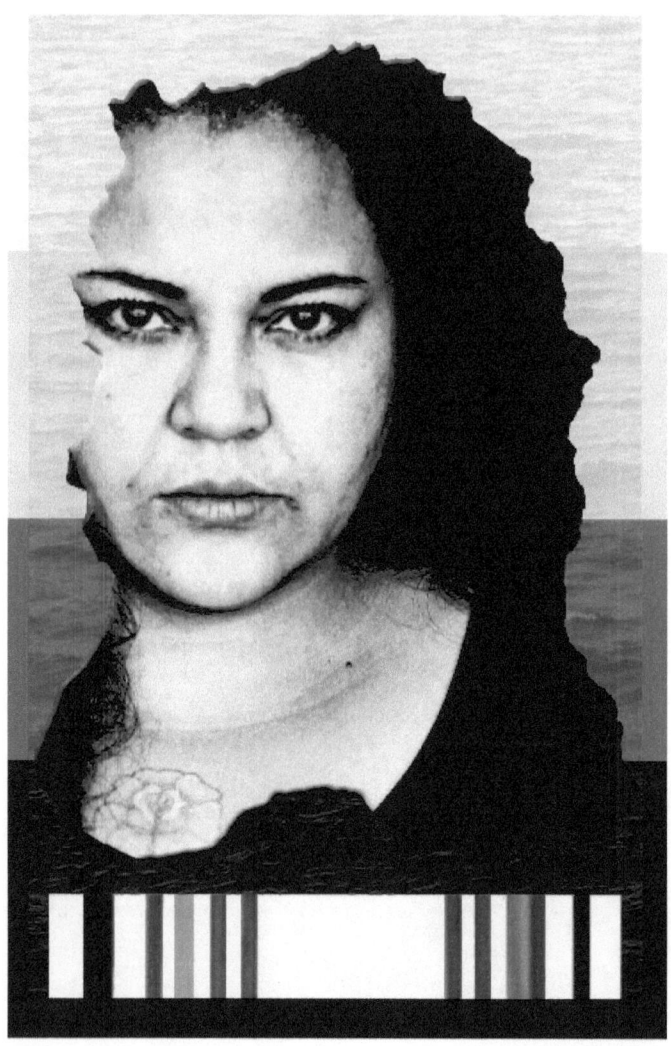

25. *Blanket*
    from the series *M: Stories of Women*
    2011

trading thereby causing destitution. At the bottom hovers a striped rectangle, like a modern bar code stamping what has been taken over, coded and sold for the gains of others. That Niro believes in the power and potential of Native women is evident here: representations of these determined, experienced women alongside their younger sisters who, accompanied by birds and butterflies, smile as they look hopefully to the future.

Originally the title of this series was *Monsters: Stories of Women*, but that seemed too extreme a statement and was modified to *M*. The original title suggests how the artist understands the way strong women are disparaged in our culture and points to her determination to develop a persuasive and positive visual vocabulary to represent women.

To this end, modern incarnations of Sky Woman function as a foundation for Niro's reconstructions of the image of First Nations women as strong, active leaders for contemporary society. Much of her work focuses on women. She begins from what she knows best – herself, her experiences and her family. Through her art Niro locates and expresses the realities of contemporary Native life in relation to her own lived experiences as a First Nations woman. Niro acknowledges the almost constant media denigration of Aboriginals, the general ignorance of the implications of long-held treaty rights and frequent experiences of racist behaviour toward First Nations people – including the horrific lack of attention to the over 1000 missing aboriginal women in Canada. This is the background against which she positions the resilience of the women in her life and in history, telling their stories with grace and humour. It seems natural to her to refuse to wallow in horror but rather to represent what people are capable of achieving, what they do in fact make of their lives, every day. There are moments, however, when she looks at her/their situation straight on and, despite a potentially light tone, makes some very strong statements. Two examples of such works are *The Shirt* (2003) and *Abnormally Aboriginal* (2013).

Produced as a five-minute video – and related series of 9 photographic prints – *The Shirt* begins from the land with views of the Grand River in winter, pans across green rolling hills and comes to rest on a native woman wearing a T-shirt and jeans, sunglasses, and her head wrapped in a bandana printed with the US flag. These alternating views of landscape and woman continue through the piece. As we move along the river's edge, huge towers carrying hydroelectric power lines dominate the background, and eventually we reach Niagara Falls, where a rainbow plays with the rushing waters. Each time we see the woman, her shirt displays a different text, first announcing *The Shirt* and then in a series of views continuing with her story as her stance becomes more confrontational:

My ancestors were annihilated exterminated murdered and massacred

They were lied to cheated tricked and deceived

Attempts were made to assimilate colonize enslave and displace them

And all's I get is this shirt

In the final view of this feisty-looking woman she has lost it all – shirt, glasses, bandana, left with only her jeans. Our last view of the shirt is on a white woman, standing happily in the landscape, the bandana around her neck

First Nations Culture Re-Imagined   53

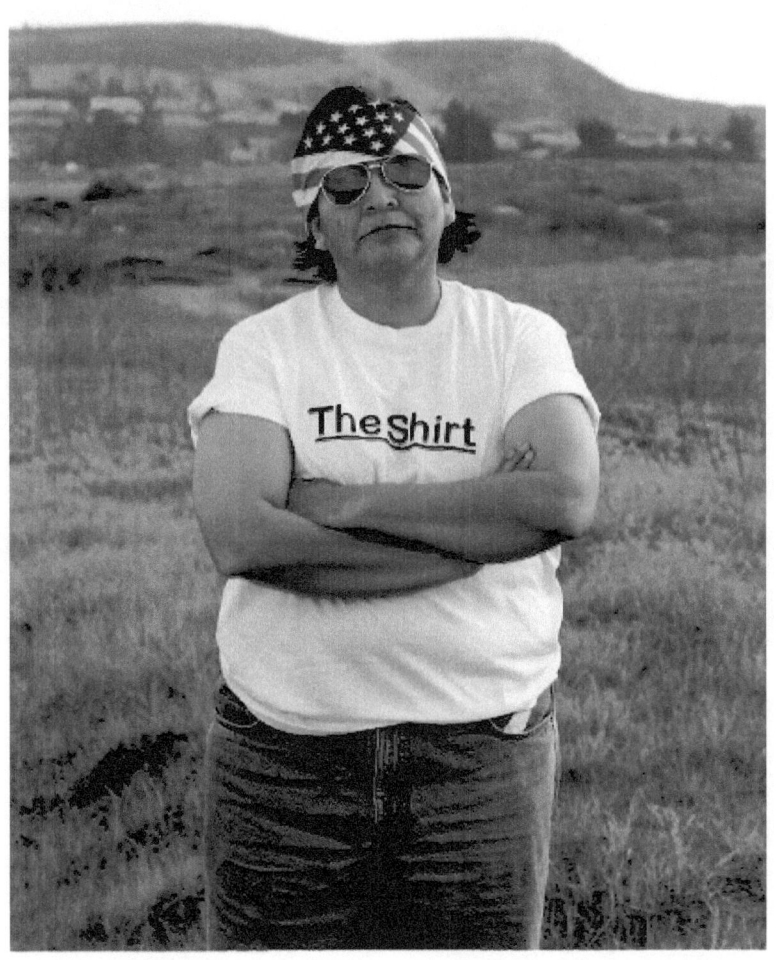

26. *The Shirt* [#1]
    2003
    series of 9 duratran prints in light boxes
    110 x 138 x 12 cm

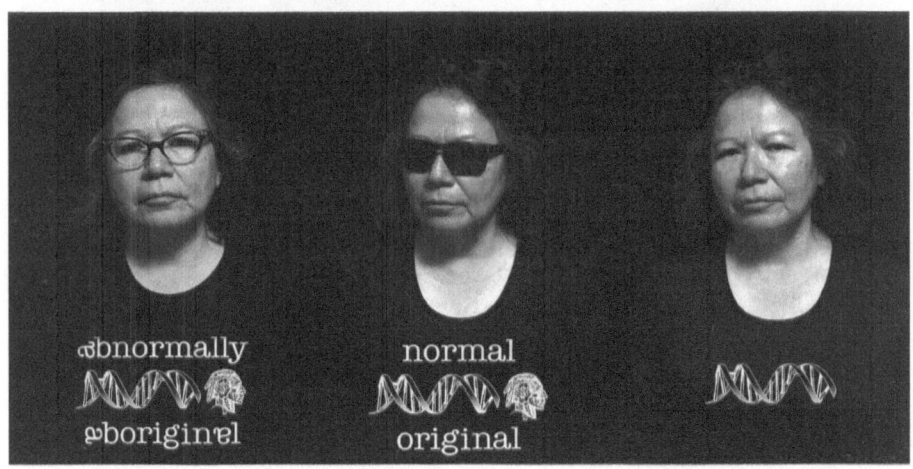

27. *Abnormally Aboriginal*
    2013
    3 digital prints
    86 x 137 x 7.5 cm [each]

and the sunglasses on her head. As the land that had been cared for in the past has been appropriated and misused, so the people who were its respectful caretakers have been stripped of their rights and livelihoods. Using the ubiquitous T-shirt to communicate this message plays against the horror of the narrative, as does the calm music of the soundtrack. The video has its humorous moments but it is also unsettling and challenging, especially since the woman is not weak and demoralized but clearly strong and defiant. Her strength parallels that of nature expressed in Niagara Falls, its power invincible.

There are different ways to convey the idea of strength. In *Abnormally Aboriginal* (2013), Niro turns the camera on herself in a large-scale self-portrait presenting three images of her across a black background. The detail in these portraits is almost brutal, her face seen very close up and filling the space; her stern expression conveys serious concern. Beneath each image is a DNA strand (recalling wampum). There is a progression to these meditations on identity. In the first image she wears glasses accompanied by the words "abnormally aboriginal"; in the second she wears sunglasses accompanied by the words "normal original"; in the third she has no glasses and there are no identifying words. Niro's comment on this work is telling:

> While I was growing up I was not aware of being an aboriginal. We were Indians. As time went by other words were added. Indigenous, Native, First Nations, and Aboriginal became the terms by which we were called and discussed. ... When I hear news coverage of "Aboriginals" now, it reminds me that others have imposed the name on us out of paternalism and misplaced sensitivity.

In contrast to the dehumanizing effect of imposed categories, Sky Woman is a liberating figure. Sky Woman frees individuals to consider their positions as humans, full of personality and centered in this place, this world.

> In an act of love, Skywoman puts herself in danger, going against rules society has set up to protect its community. In that one unselfish act she loses her way and ultimately everything. She floats through darkness for what seems like an endless amount of time. She doesn't know where she is going or how long she will be in this state. Her fear eventually is overcome by curiosity. She begins to look forward to a new life with her unborn child, in a new and distant land.[16]

IV. Great Peace and the Message of Peacemaker

In addition to Sky Woman, another important legend for Niro is Peacemaker, an historical figure who embodies the founding of the Confederacy of the Iroquois Nations. In a time of violent conflict among the Five Nations (Mohawk, Oneida, Onondaga, Cayuga and Seneca[17]), thought to have occurred in the 15th century, tradition holds that the Creator sent a messenger of peace who proposed the Great Law of Peace and a legal system of self-rule. Born to a young Huron woman near the Bay of Quinte, the baby seemed special but was rejected by his mother. He survived all attempts to kill him and as an adult he left the community that rejected him to pursue his goal to bring people together in Great Peace. In one story we are told that Peacemaker travelled to the Mohawks in a canoe of white stone, which astonished everyone by floating on the water.

In his bid to convince warring peoples to accept his ideas, Peacemaker (Deganawidah) influenced several special individuals. One was Jikonsaheh [also spelled Jigosase] (Cat-Faced Woman), who was an elder living in isolation on a riverbank in what is now western New York State. She provided a neutral area for warriors to meet and put aside their weapons. Because she was feeding and aiding the warriors, Peacemaker asked her to hear him and his message that all people are to live in Peace and Unity with the entire natural world. Recognizing the

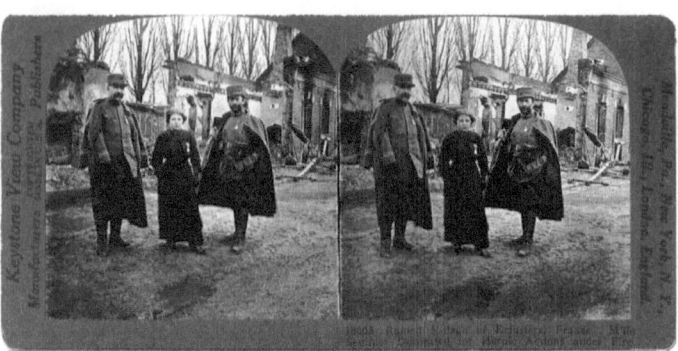
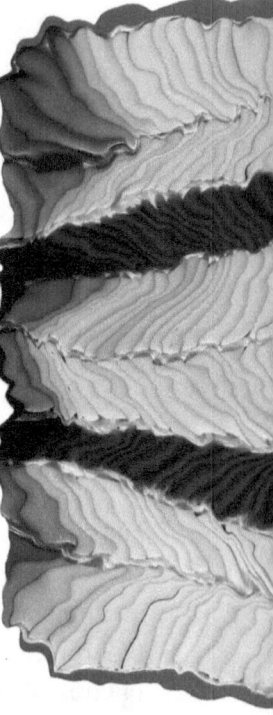

First Nations Culture Re-Imagined

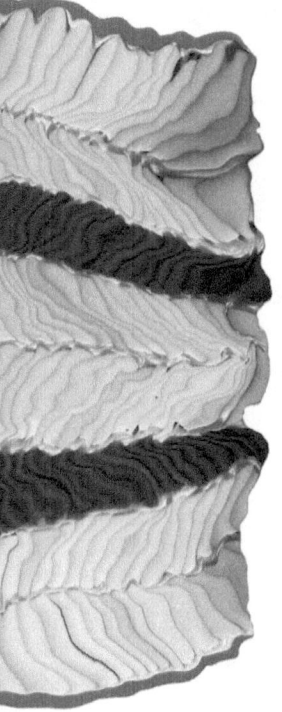
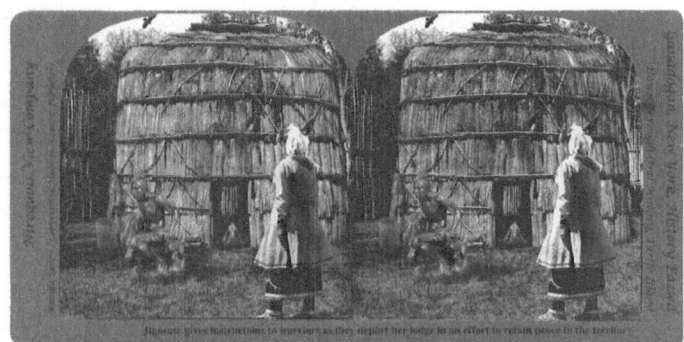

28. *Parallel Worlds of Women and Warriors*
    2010
    digital print
    312 x 109 cm

wisdom of Peacemaker's ideas she accepted the message of peace, becoming a powerful leader and symbol of the Clan Mothers of the Iroquois Nations (sometimes called the Peace Queen).

For Niro Jikonsaheh is a courageous, independent woman equal to any warrior or leader. In *Parallel Worlds of Women and Warriors* (2010) Niro juxtaposes representations of the legendary Native woman – suggested by a figure resembling a traditional cornhusk doll – and an historical young French woman, Mlle Semper, who resisted the advance of German soldiers in World War I. The two images, both presented as nineteenth-century stereocard photographs (and accompanying narrative texts), are separated by a digitally manipulated image of a two row wampum belt that seems to explode – the traditional white and purple shells morphed into a white, red and blue form that references not only wampum but also a female sensuality that echoes recent feminist art.[18] The unusual wampum colours relate to the French tricolore (or the American flag), supporting the political message of the work. The medium and format make the message contemporary, like a vivid news bulletin bringing forward the portraits of the roles of women that are usually ignored. Niro recognizes in the stories of both Jikonsaheh and Mlle Semper messages of peace that spark the imagination.

The story of Peacemaker includes accounts of various relationships, one of the most significant of which is his interactions with Hiawatha (Hyenwatha). Hiawatha was inconsolable, a man in deep grief for his family who through jealousy had been killed by members of his community. Peacemaker created the Condolence ceremony to relieve Hiawatha's grief, a ritual process that includes singing, hair combing and the creation of wampum (using white-shell beads found in the bed of a lake). Together

Peacemaker and Hiawatha approached a leader who refused to accept the Great Law of Peace, the isolated, evil Tadodarho (a wild man noted for the snakes in his hair, cannibalism and the crookedness of his body) and eventually convinced him to accept the Peace. Teaching him how to eat and take proper care of himself so that his body straightened, Hiawatha also combed the snakes from his hair. The Peacemaker made Tadodarho responsible for the Fire. Eventually all Five Nations accepted the Great Law of Peace, each giving an arrow that were bound together by Peacemaker as a symbol of one great power.[19]

Many of the themes and material found in the Peacemaker narrative can be seen in Niro's work. In *The Essential Sensuality of Ceremony* (2002) she takes up the notion of grief and the value of ritual to work through despair and reach out again to life. Five large-scale black and white photographs depict in close-up views a young grieving man who is offered solace by a woman. The ritual involves: singing, laying on of hands, burning tobacco, wiping away tears of grief so that he can think with a clear mind and providing nutrition. The rituals represented here parallel those of Peacemaker's Condolence Ritual as he drew Hiawatha out of inconsolable grief and brought Tadodarho back to a reasonable life. Niro meditates on the challenges of contemporary life for Native people who face loss on every hand – of dignity, status, land and language – and as a consequence suffer grief and confusion. Her work makes visible the value of Native traditions and customs. The beauty of these photographs balanced in light and shadows, as well as the direct yet delicate presentation of emotions of the images, bring the viewer close to this experience.

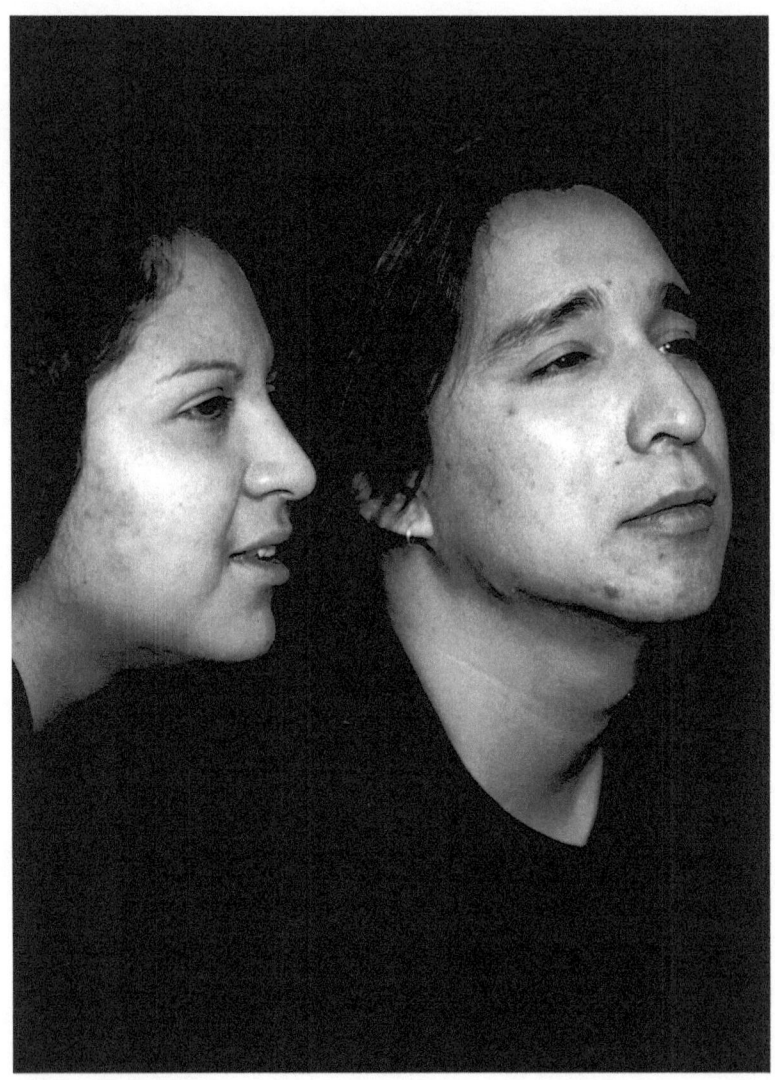

29. *The Essential Sensuality of Ceremony* [singing]
    2002
    black and white photograph
    101.6 x 127 cm

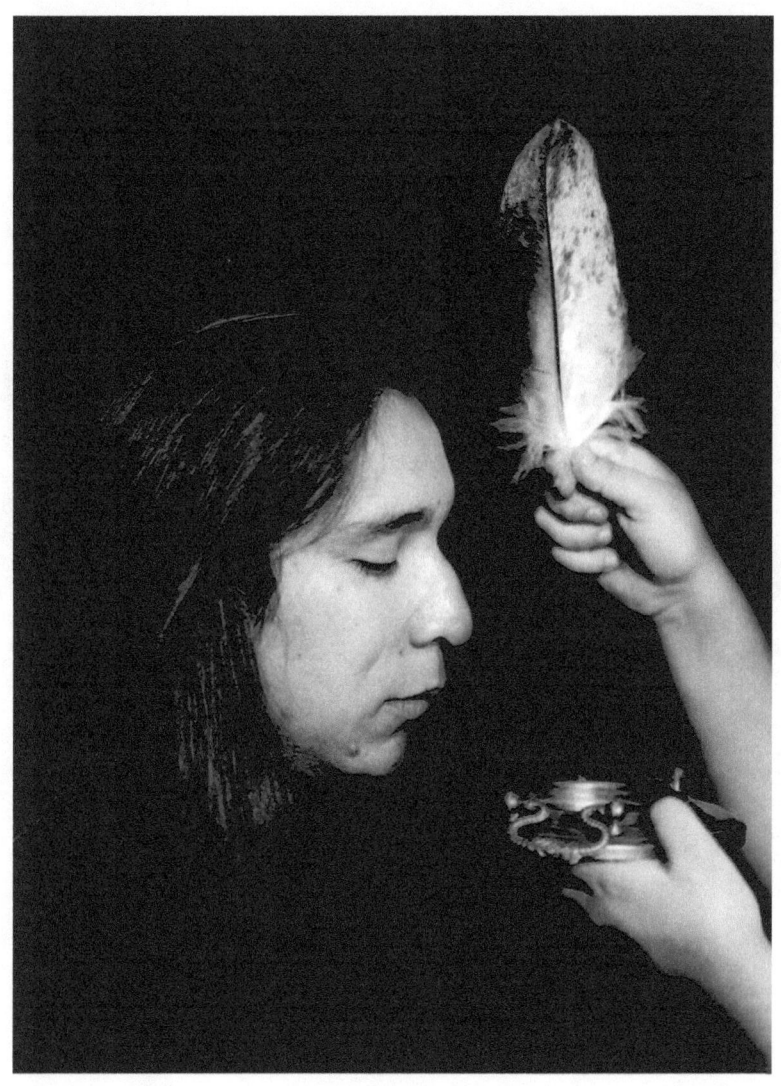

30. *The Essential Sensuality of Ceremony* [burning tobacco] 2002

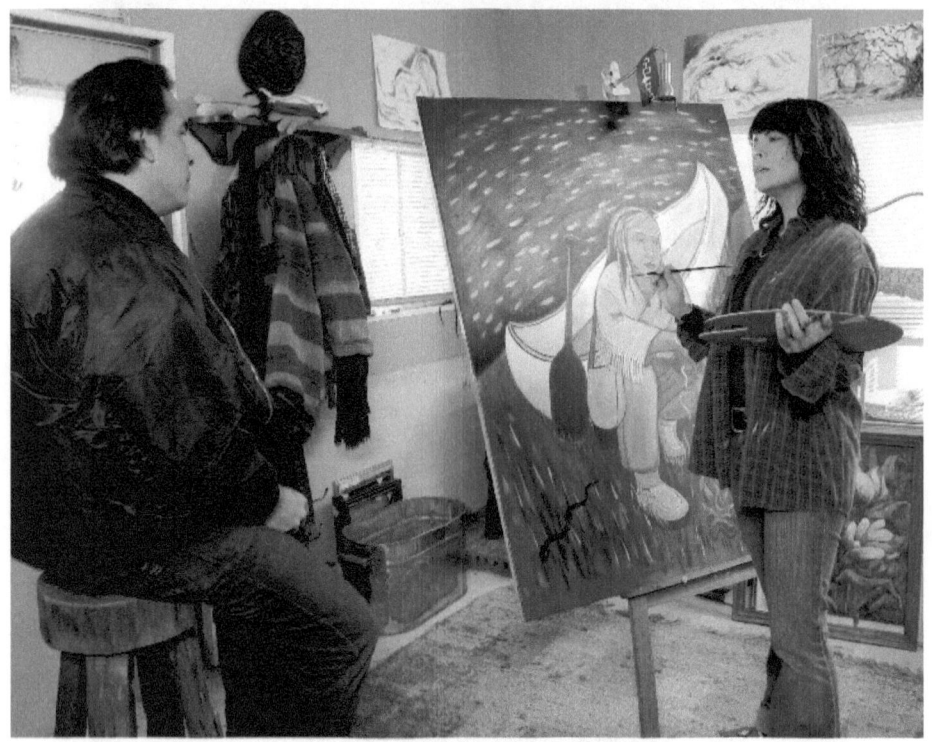

31. *Kissed by Lightning* [production still]
    2009
    HD video, colour
    90 minutes
    photograph courtesy of Calvin Thomas

The concern with overarching grief and its effects is central to one of the most powerful expressions of Niro's response to the Peacemaker story: her 2009 film *Kissed by Lightning*. The central character in the film is Mavis Dogblood, an artist who is mourning the death of her husband, Jessie Lightning. We watch her experience the pain over and over again, following her journey as she gradually accepts the loss and can look forward in her life. The other characters revolve around her, responding to her intense grief in different ways. From her own experiences, Niro evokes various types of people and the situations present in the lives of Natives.

For example, Mavis is completing a series of paintings (actually Niro's own works) based on the Peacemaker story that her husband had told her, preparing for an exhibition to be held at a New York gallery. Her friend Bug, who deeply cares for her, is the one who articulates the central theme of the film. In a series of central episodes, the two are driving a van with her paintings to New York from her home on the reserve near Toronto. After a fraught border crossing into the United States, they continue through a snow filled winter landscape that brings back Bug's memories of a trip he took with his mother and sister. He reminisces about that bus trip, tracing Peacemaker's steps from Lake Ontario into what is now New York State, saying how amazing he finds it that one person could have had such significant influence. Mavis questions this and he expands on what Peacemaker provided – because of his philosophy the Iroquois Confederacy came into being and the Condolence Ceremony was developed. "Think about it," he urges her; "how terrible it is to feel such inner turmoil, to have no reason to live." As Bug looks at the passing landscape he voices his belief: "when our feet touch the earth our souls mix with the souls of our ancestors."

The ancestors are present in the film, literally as well as through a number of references and devices – one of which is music, which plays a major role in the narrative. During her flashbacks, Mavis sees her husband playing his viola and talking about the music he is writing. He tells her: "incredible harmonies rush through me all the time." We see him standing in the snow with a powerful landscape behind him, playing the viola with tremendous intensity and emotion. In a different way, the idea of ancestors and song is introduced when Mavis and Bug stop for lunch in a small-town restaurant in New York State. The place is full of objects that convey stereotyped messages, including a large wooden 'Indian' complete with headdress and tomahawk, along with the frowning white clientele and server. As they eat, an outspoken and friendly group of African-Americans arrive from New York City on their way to Buffalo. They are amazed to discover these two Mohawks: "you are not all dead yet," they marvel. "And here you are on your homeland," they announce. They serenade the two with a special song including the refrain "Thank you God for the Mohawk people!" Mavis finally gives in to their request for one of her people's songs, describing it as one her husband used to sing her and the only one she knows. Its lyrics question the location of home and the singer promises never to leave again. Now it is the African-Americans who talk about their ancestors, who live in them and sing through them. Thus in this scene, filled with humour, Niro draws parallels between two peoples who have suffered yet persist in their goals to construct a meaningful life based on their histories.

Kissed by Lightning is consistent in the ways that setting, sound track and narrative communicate and enhance the film's message, which is a vivid account of

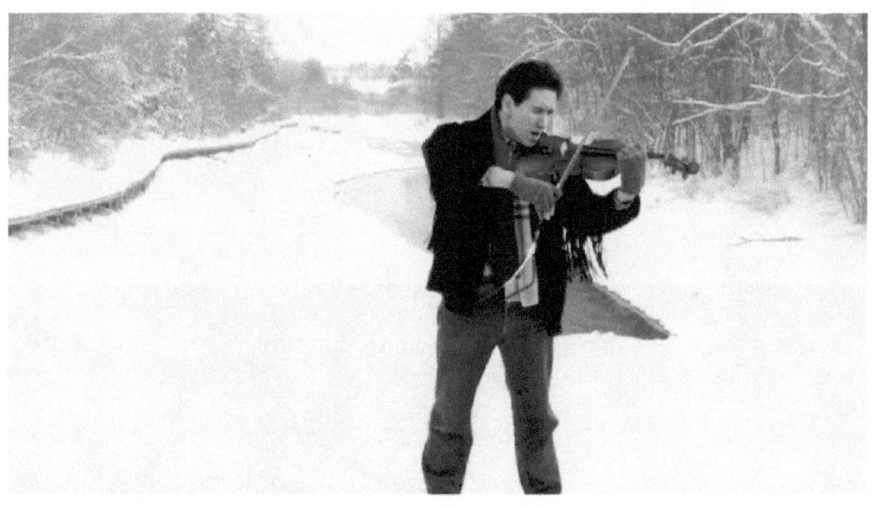

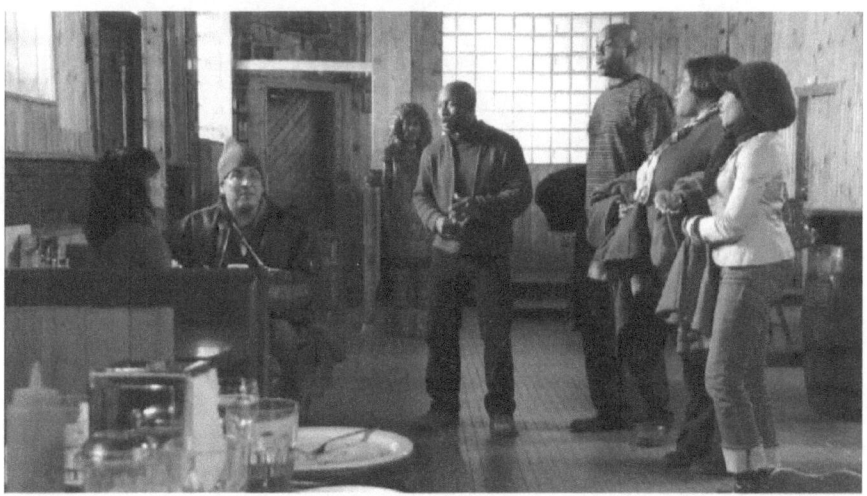

32. *Kissed by Lightning* [film stills]
    2009

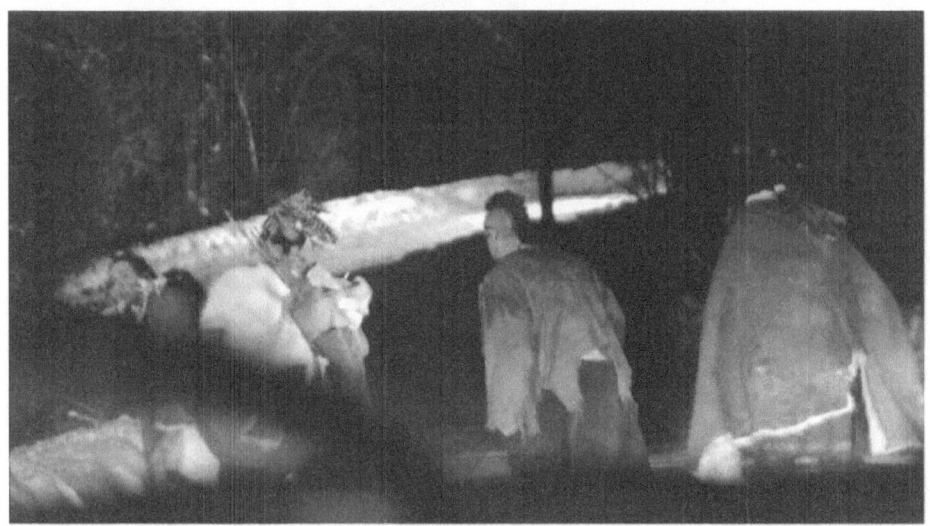

33. *Kissed by Lightning* [film still]
    2009

the belief system of the Haudenosaunee that is based in large part on the ideals of the Peacemaker. References to the legend are played out through dream scenes – at one point we see Hiawatha approaching the evil Tadodarho, at another point Bug's ancestors stand behind his mother who has arrived to help him when he has been injured – and through brief appearances in the real space of the main characters. Thus, in a night scene when Mavis and Bug realize they are lost on a wooded road, they stop the van and discuss how they might find their way back to the right highway. Suddenly a group of Native men, Mohawk warriors in traditional dress, appear from the trees and walk in front of the van. As they move they exchange glances with the couple looking out at them and keep walking into the bush where they disappear. Startled, Mavis exclaims: "Did you see that?" and Bug responds: "I think they're lost." It is an eerie moment with clear personal and cultural reverberations: to the people of the past who lived in this region; to their history of loss of homeland; to contemporary First Nations who are psychically lost.

V. Decoding Memory

Shelley Niro's whole body of work resonates with this deep sense of loss. In response, she excavates the richness of cultural and personal memory, proposing multiple routes to wholeness within the Iroquois traditions. Niro searches her own photographic archives to trace her formative roots – as we see in *This Land is Mime Land*. For Mavis Dogblood in *Kissed by Lightning*, an encounter with her late husband's mother in her home filled with family photographs and souvenirs of her ancestors helps her to accept loss and move forward with her life. For Niro and for her pregnant daughter Naoga, taking on the guise of Sky Woman is empowering and reassuring – an ideal expressed in the series *M: Stories of Women*.

Through her art Niro presents herself as a decoder of layers of past experience. This role is powerfully evident in her painting *Seeing With My Memory* (2000). Here her source and foundation is Nature. She stands in a brilliant landscape, next to a tree with one hand resting on the trunk that seems to glow with tongues of fire. Everything in the landscape vibrates with energy – the hill that rolls down to the river rushing around islands; trees dotted with leaves in designs reminiscent of beadwork; blue sky streaked with wind-swept clouds. Niro stares intently into our world, a determined figure in her jean jacket, a poppy pinned to the collar, embodying the values entrusted to her by her father,

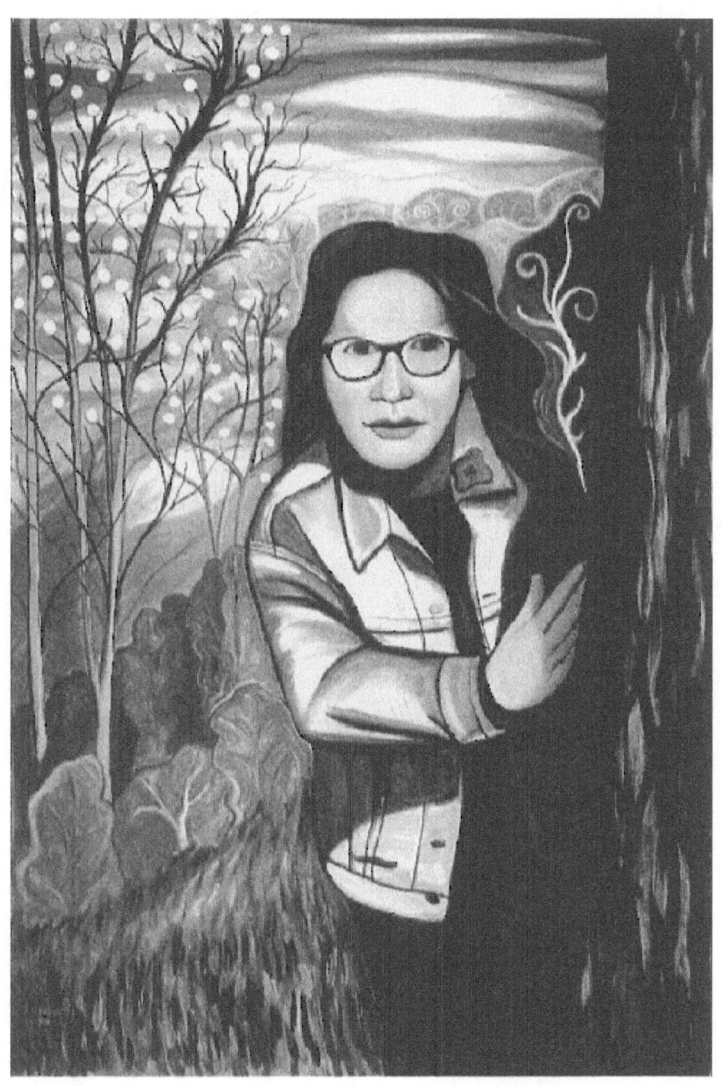

34. *Seeing With My Memory*
    2000
    oil on canvas
    103.6 x 152.4 cm
    photograph courtesy of Cees Van Gemerden

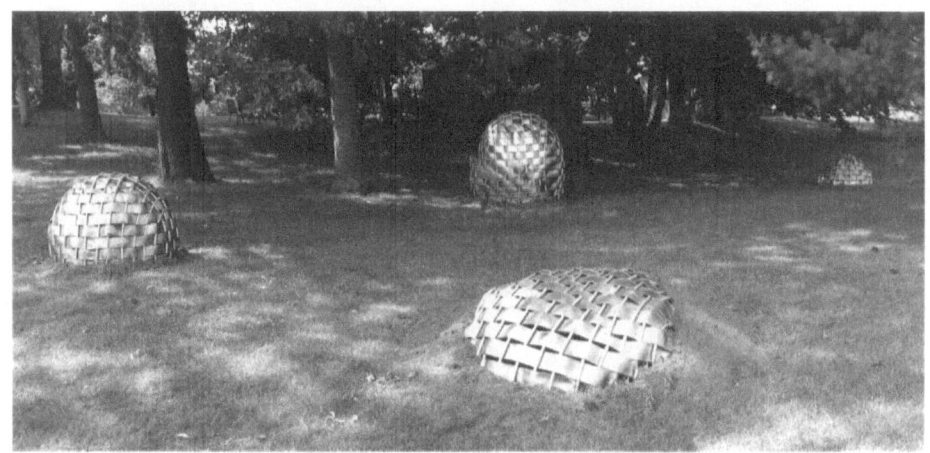

35. *Basket Series*
    installation at the Woodland Cultural Centre, Six Nations, Brantford
    2012
    rubber tubing, wood frames, silver paint
    dimensions variable

translating them for future generations.

Playing with the significance of the land, Niro's installation *Basket Series* (2012) encodes a message that is a key to her work. Set in a green lawn among trees, four large woven silver baskets seem to force their way out of the earth. They are like archetypal forms emerging from sacred land, bringing a history of basket weaving into the future – sleek rounded shapes whose silver surface suggests a space odyssey, a constellation for the 21st century. There is a monumental quality to this grouping of silver baskets that demands serious consideration. The artist seems to use the craft of basket weaving that was practiced for centuries by Native peoples, especially women, to signify the submerged memories and histories that through her career she has referenced in different forms and materials.

Notes

1. Shelley Niro, cited in the blog post *Kayeriakweks. Shelley Niro*. http://Kayeriakweks.wordpress.com/2012/11/04/shelley-niro/. Accessed November 12, 2012.

2. Information from Shelley Niro from conversations with the author over the months of July to November 2012, unless otherwise noted.

3. Bruce Elliott Johansen and Barbara Alice Mann, eds., *Encyclopedia of the Haudenosaunee (Iroquois Confederacy)* (Westport: Greenwood Press, 2000), 325-28.

4. "I think printmaking is much like sculpture. You have to conceive of an idea and build on that idea a layer at a time. Photography is more immediate and serves a different kind of purpose for myself." Shelley Niro. Private correspondence, March 11, 2014.

5. The series was exhibited in *Mohawks in Beehives + Other Works* at Mercer Union in 1992, her first show in Toronto.

6. Shelley Niro, *An Essential Personal Journey Through Iroquois Myths, Legends, Icons and History*, M.F.A. Thesis (London, University of Western Ontario, 1997),

26. This document can be accessed through a link in the bibliography on Niro's website: www.shelleyniro.ca

7. Allan J. Ryan, *The Trickster Shift* (Vancouver and Seattle: University of British Columbia Press and University of Washington Press, 1999), 66.

8. Doug George-Kanentiio, *Iroquois Culture & Commentary* (Sante Fe: Clear Light Publishers, 2000), 53-55. See also W.G. Spittal, ed., *Iroquois Women An Anthology* (Ohsweken: IPACS, 1990), especially pages 136-40 and 183-87.

9. Joseph Brant (1742-1807) was an important Mohawk leader and ally of the British during the American Revolution. His history has a mixed impact for First Nations, some believing he was not true to his heritage. However, there is a city named for him in Ontario and a significant monument in his honour (1866).

10. Ruth B. Phillips, *Trading Identities: the Souvenir in Native North American Art from the Northeast, 1700-1900* (Seattle: University of Washington Press, 1998), 277-78, and Heather Norris Nicholson, "Making Things Happen Through Parody and Visual Irony: Reflecting on the Work of Shelley Niro," in *Screening Culture: Constructing Image and Identity*, ed. H.N. Nicholson (Lanham: Lexington Books, 2003), 157-68. Phillips and Nicholson include significant discussions of the film in these publications that directly influenced my discussion here.

11. Johansen and Mann, eds., *Encyclopedia of the Haudenosaunee*, 85-88.

12. Barbara Alice Mann, *Iroquoian Women: The Gantowisas* (New York: Peter Lang, 2000), 3; 5.

13. Shelley Niro, cited in blog post, Michelle Murdock, *Shelley Niro's Skywoman Series*, Fenimore Art Museum (Tuesday, June 2, 2009). http://fenimoreartmuseum.blogspot.ca/2009/06/by-michelle-murdock-curator-of.html. Accessed November 12, 2012.

14. Johansen and Mann, eds., *Encyclopedia of the Haudenosaunee*, 53. The legend holds that when Sky Woman died, her head was thrown into the sky and became Grandmother Moon, reflecting light at night, regulating the monthly cycles of all female life that guarantees new life.

15. In September 2009 Health Canada shipped dozens of body bags to several remote First Nations communities in Manitoba, which had been hard-hit by the H1N1 flu in the spring. While Health Minister Leona Aglukkaq was quick to express her ignorance and concern for this clearly insensitive response, the disturbing message that was sent to the people of these communities caused much concern about the promises of the Federal government to help prepare for the flu. Chief David Harper of Northern Manitoba's Garden Hill reserve was quoted at the time as saying: "This says to me they've given up."

16. Shelley Niro, *M: Stories of Women* [exhibition catalogue] (Toronto: Gallery 44, 2011).

17. With the addition of the Tuscarora in 1722, the Five Nations became what we now refer to as the Six Nations.

18. Jolene Rickard, "Personal Risk," in *Counting Coup*, ed. Ryan Rice (Santa Fe: Institute of American Indian Art: Museum of Contemporary Native Art, 2011), 22. Rickard cites Judy Chicago's installation *The Dinner Party* as a reference.

19. Janet C. Berlo & Ruth B. Phillips, *Native North American Art* (Oxford: Oxford University Press, 1998), 93-94. *American Indians: First People of America and Canada – Turtle Island*, "Native American Legends: The Peacemaker and the Tree of Peace," http://www.firstpeople.us . Accessed November 10, 2012.

Conversation with Shelley Niro
July 27, 2012

Madeline Lennon—Shelley, how did you decide to be an artist?

Shelley Niro—Being an artist was always encouraged at home, especially by my father, and from a really young age. It wasn't me specifically, but he always had us sketching. He would show us something and say, draw this tree; this is how you show perspective in the landscape, and the one who does the best tree will get a quarter! So okay, working hard, trying to get the tree drawn. But you were always busy doing something like that. My parents – because we were pretty poor, we had no money or anything, so they always had to figure out ways we could work together to try to make money as a family. And it came down to making stuff, making necklaces and selling them at fairs, powwows and generally places where we could set up shop and sell stuff. And then it was soapstone carving – we all had a chunk of soapstone and carved away. We didn't get rich off it but we made enough to buy a pair of jeans or something. There was that element of trying to provide through the means that we had.

At some point I decided that I didn't want to make that kind of art or craft. I knew I could do it if I had to, but I wanted to keep exploring. That's where my mother comes in. She was able to create things that went beyond craft. She was an artist who could make something that was a little bit different and had its own personality. Also, living on the reserve, I think everyone was an artist. Everyone had their own skills – people could draw, people could do watercolour – really delicate little watercolours you'd see, of people dressed in traditional outfits that had a really particular look to it. You'd think: these are real artists. They know how to make things. There are people who could make drums or rattles, moccasin people and people who did bead work. It seemed like everyone would do something. So it wasn't such a strange thing to do traditional things. The strange thing is when you say I'm going to go over here and do something different with the same technique. And of course my parents could never understand why I would want to do that. "You can't sell that!"

So I was brought up in that environment that started out as providing but then turned into something else.

ML—How old would you have been when you realized that you wanted to do this differently?

SN—I think I was about twelve or so – that I knew that I wanted to make stuff – that I didn't want to make the thing that was going to be expected that I would make. I knew I had a strong desire to draw and paint but I didn't want to do it just because I could. I thought I had to find my way to that world and try to figure out what the subject would be or what's important for me to want to say and I wanted to take that really seriously. I did not want to just start making pretty things just because. It took a long time for me to get to that point, and I was thirty when I decided, okay, I really have to do this now. So I was quite a bit older than a lot of people who start out being artists.

ML—It sounds like it's not that you weren't an artist, but that you were trying to decide what that meant to you, to be an artist.

SN—Yes, I just didn't want to take it lightly. All along I'd been learning, taking drawing classes. I was never satisfied with my drawing. So I just kept doing it until I could be happy with what I am doing, but I never found that happiness – but I keep trying. It's something that is a talent – putting down what you see. I keep trying to grab onto it. I am still working on it. I don't think I'll ever get to that point, when I can say "I can draw!"

Painting is a whole different can of worms. I feel really competent painting. It's something that is more natural for me. I just can't figure it out – why can I not be happy with my drawings.

ML—This is interesting because some say that painting is almost a form of drawing, but with colour, though of course the technique is different.

SN—Pretty different and it feels like sculpture in a way, painting, because you can build the colour up. When I think of drawing I think – wow how did they do that. To a point where you want to stay within that photograph frame, exploring the shadows and depth and texture. I like that. But I'll never get there.

ML—It is really interesting to hear about your childhood and how art was part of your community, and still is. In an early part of your film *Suite: INDIAN* (2005) it is the creative people you feature and what they are doing, and you realize the people were doing this centuries ago. And they are still doing it and it still has value (not just monetary) and represents a certain attitude and acceptance of culture and cultural production.

SN—I wanted to celebrate the different art forms in the community and show the people that championed their specialty, and to give a bit of a showcase. It is just a bit, because there are tons more and many different crafts and arts that people make.

ML—Your parents' influence seems very important. They both sound like they had artistic qualities and they encouraged all of you to do these things. Do people now continue to do this – do they teach others on the reserve, or do people learn from looking.

SN—It's become more of the curriculum in the school. They learn how to do things in a much more structured way now. My sister was the doll maker in the film. She gives workshops in schools. My daughter has learned how to make cornhusk dolls. She goes into high schools and gives workshops. She finds it funny – she goes into a high school class, boys and girls and they come into class like real teenagers. But when she shows them how to make them, they all get really quiet and work diligently on their dolls. This is amazing – teenage boys working on a doll! They are aware of what this means historically and they want to learn. They are invested in the connection this gives them to a lot of things.

Conversation with Shelley Niro 83

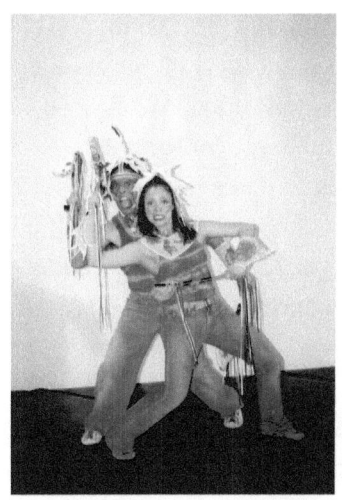

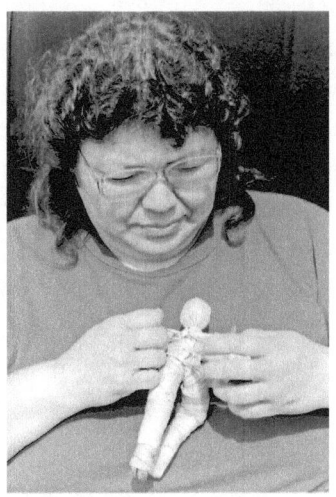

36. *Suite: INDIAN* [details of film stills]
    2005
    mini DV, HD cam, 16 mm, colour
    60 minutes
    photograph of dancers courtesy of Brenda Mitten

And I think that it is not perfect yet but they have language schools on the reserve and so they are learning the language. And many of these things are coming into the community. People are aware of what's not there and trying to make it part of everybody's life.

ML—Thank you. Let's talk now about the reality of you being a woman artist who is also a First Nations woman.

SN—When I first started exhibiting at the Woodland Cultural Centre through their First Nations art exhibition, I went there and found three women artists in quite a large group maybe around 54 – all those men and three women! And I thought why? What's going on here? The male imagery in the show as I remember was all warriors and heroes, and the women were dancers, and I thought it left a lot of spaces empty and open. And I thought as a woman artist what am I going to do about this? So I quietly committed myself to making art that spoke about women and tried to create work that showed women in a realistic way. That's where I incorporate a lot of images of women that are not models; they are not anything like that, but people you find in everyday ordinary life. And I also thought at that time it felt like you needed positive reinforcement of women as well. What I was seeing was really small and usually Indian women are depicted in a negative way, so I thought okay, this is one of the areas that I am going to work on.

ML—That comes across again in the *Suite: INDIAN* series, and in your use of Sky Woman that is so powerful.

SN—Sky Woman is such an amazing story. To me it's imagination. This story was told – people can't put a time on it – the stories have been in the community for millennia. And I think about people who make up a story about a woman who comes from the sky. She comes from a place where everything is brightly lit, they've never seen darkness. By accident she ends up falling through a hole. There is more to the story, but just seeing that image of this other world that is up in the sky and there is no disease or death – did someone think this up and tell it? It conjures up all kinds of stuff, it can be interpreted, reinterpreted, it can be used in so many ways as a metaphor for life itself. She falls through the hole and it is all about the diaspora, falling from one place to another place. She has to think of the consequences and has to change, learn the new rules about coming to a new place. So I think it is striking – you can use the story over and over, and reinterpret it in your own ways. It plays an important part because I think this story was told so many years ago and here we are 2012 and elements can still be brought to this time period and reinterpreted. And it's such a good film script! It's a narrative and I don't think I could ever get tired of the story.

ML—It becomes so personal. You have talked about your daughter at the end of her pregnancy and you turned her into Sky Woman – and it is so contemporary.

SN—That's one story, and I keep thinking that's the last time I will use that story – there are other stories I can use. I have to do that and look at other stories.

ML—Yes, but somehow I think you will never completely let go of this. The whole business with tobacco and

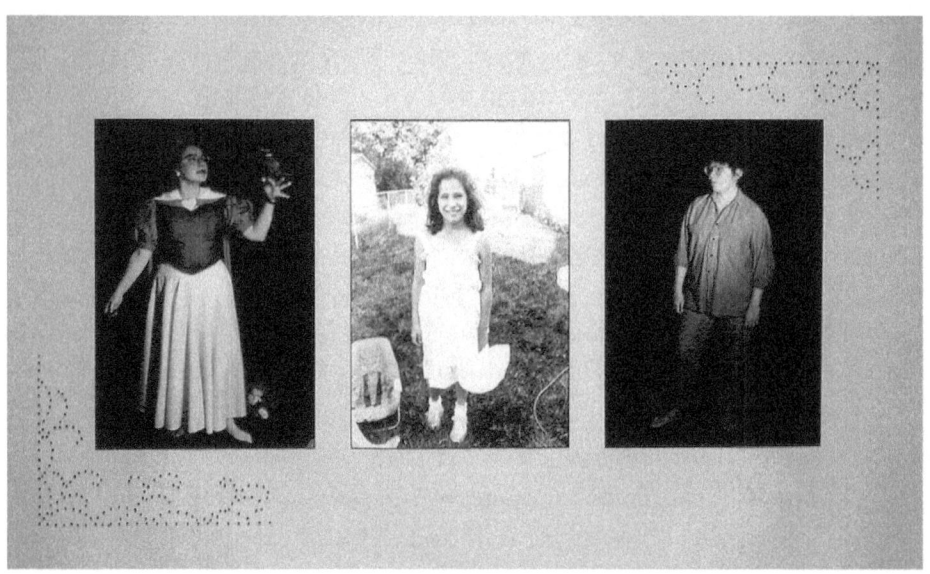

37. *Warning*
    from the series *This Land is Mime Land*
    1992
    hand-tinted gelatin silver prints in hand-drilled overmat
    94 x 56 cm
    National Gallery of Canada/Musée des beaux-arts du Canada, Ottawa
    Photo © National Gallery of Canada/Musée des beaux-arts du Canada

strawberries – so many issues of life it takes up, the land, ecology, along with the woman issue.

SN—There are always contemporary stories to consider too – like the murdered and missing 500 women, and now the number is the missing 600 women. It can be really depressing if you think of those connections. How do you move forward and incorporate those stories as well, without exploiting the stories of these women. It becomes a balancing act of how I tell the Sky Woman story and the missing women. I've done a little bit in *M: Stories of Women* (2011) but it becomes such a personal struggle. How do you do it without having it seem that you are making pop art out of a tragedy? It bugs me when I see people act as though they know all about it and make art out of it.

ML—It seems to me that it is not just with Sky Woman that we have a sense of women in the culture. In one of your works that is so widely seen, *This Land is Mime Land* (1992), it is not just as a woman that you speak. I can see why you are compared with other artists who take on personas, such as Cindy Sherman. But I see this as quite different because it is not just you but it's also your history, and the use of archival photos from your family to comment on who you are – that is also about being a woman in the cultures that you work in.

SN—There are also designs on the mats that surround the photographs. When I was making that piece I was really invested in beadwork as being an expressive component of women's work. Because when I was growing up people who did bead work were looked at as selling out, or making tourist art, that sort of thing.

Again, people would bead stuff and put dates on it and sell it. It had this connotation that people who did that were making stuff for tourists.

As I started working through that whole process of looking at women's work, I thought, well, it has to go beyond. Even though women make this work to sell it to live, it can go on to become something else. My father used to buy bead work from an old woman if he wanted to get a special gift for somebody. We'd go to her house. She was almost blind – if you do bead work it wrecks your eyes – she was almost blind then. He looked at this bead work as though it was so special. She was the only one doing it – she was like a small treasure in the community. That shows a lot – no one was doing anything, so he would buy this bead work from her. But now bead work is a big to-do.

It was in the early 60s, before Indians had rights. I grew up with the idea that people are not doing this, and when I was more mature, I decided to make up my own designs for beadwork – and then people would say, that's not a traditional design. But I thought that at some point the designs were quite contemporary – somebody had to make them up. And because I was only using mat boards and a dremmel drill, I made my own designs and tried to make them look like beadwork.

It was really kind of fun. I didn't have to stick with the traditional, I could make them up. I opened a small door for myself. So I went on with that project and made a design for each frame. That was my big bridging work incorporating images of my mother and my daughter, old photographs I had of my father's grandmother and my mother's aunt – people that I knew who they were but didn't know them. I have my

Conversation with Shelley Niro

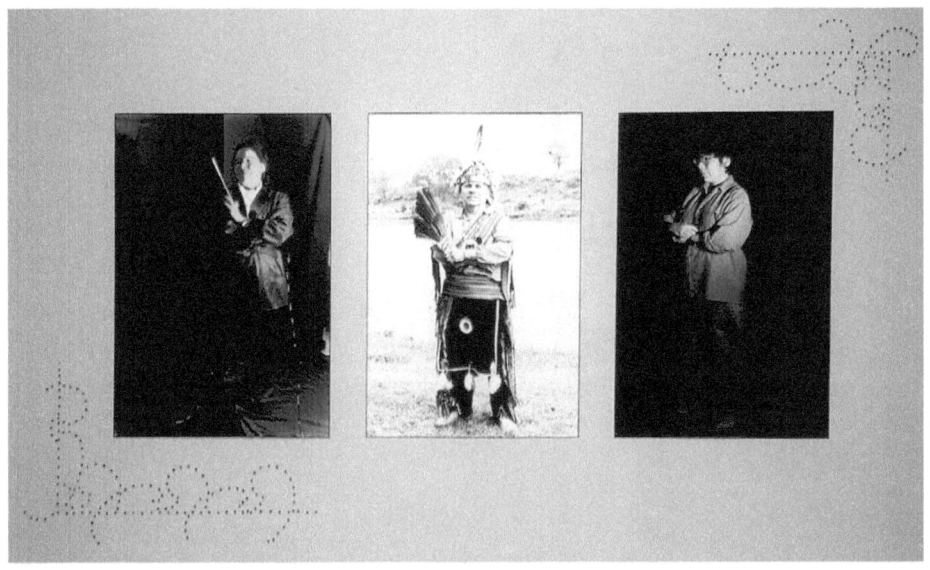

38. *Always A Gentleman*
    from the series *This Land is Mime Land*
    1992
    National Gallery of Canada/Musée des beaux-arts du Canada, Ottawa
    Photo © National Gallery of Canada/Musée des beaux-arts du Canada

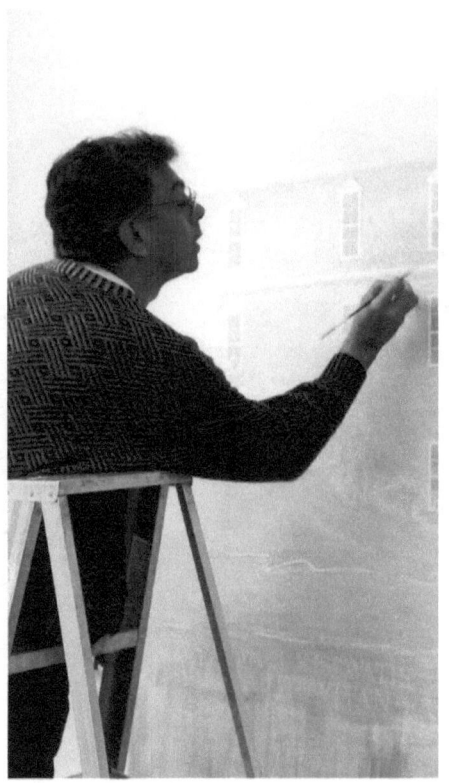

39. *Robert's Paintings* [detail of film still]
    2011
    HD video, colour
    52 minutes

father in there too in some of the images – he is 17 in one and in the other he is 70.

ML—Do you have any other thoughts on this topic, about women and art?

SN—I really directed my work that way. Almost secondary though, I started including men in my work in *Robert's Paintings* (2011). Once in a presentation someone said I notice you are starting to include men in your work, is there a reason? I don't know, menopause? There was not a peep, no laughter, and I thought, uh oh. But I try not to be so female centric, because that has connotations.

It's about creating a balance. I made myself aware that women have to have representation, and if I am going to use that representation in my art work it is a good thing. And now that I am opening it up to male representation too I am not as female centric as I used to be.

I also believe it is creating a balance. I like to include the male presence more and more.

ML—Certainly you do focus on male characters in some of your films, in *Honey Moccasin* (1998) and in *Kissed by Lightning* (2009). The women are important but the men have a significant role to play as well. And gender issues come up. So your approach is getting broader and reflecting our times.

SN—There aren't too many Native films about relationships. If you've seen Native films, Native characters are stereotyped. Anything about Native people on reserves has everyone drinking, with limited morals and no conscience about consequences. It almost makes them look like they are thoughtless and directionless.

I am doing it little bit by little bit. I didn't want it to become: 'The Relationship'. Okay, now we'll do something on men and women. Even that feels kind of funny, because sometimes when you see it in a film I think that's way too much information. I just wanted to do it very quietly so that it becomes a connection between the male and the female. A few people commented that they'd never seen a loving relationship on film between men and women before and they really appreciate that area being explored. I think it is really important too. It has to become like role modeling. Not that I am a big expert on that either!

ML — Your life and your experiences are important.

SN — It's always a challenge, because you want to do something realistically and keep it within that normal realm. In *Kissed by Lightning* and in *Suite: INDIAN* – in the dance pieces where we see Santee Smith she is alone and in the next piece she is dancing with the male figure behind her. It's all about support, he is there to support her and he is mirroring her and he gives her that strength that she needs to carry on.

In *Kissed by Lightning* I really wanted to show that the female is quite capable of being on her own, but the male character will come in and enriches the environment and brings his own knowledge and strength and it makes it a much more powerful environment than when she is alone.

ML — We've talked a lot about women. There is something else so present in your work – the land, the Grand

River. We once had a conversation about the Adirondacks as Mohawk territory. What is this in your work?

SN — My dad always used to talk about the Mohawk Valley. "Oh I heard the Mohawk Valley is beautiful." He talked about it in such a way that it seemed to be a mythological place. So when you put it in your mind that way it feels like its Shangri-La or so far away you can't get to it, but it has this memory. When I was close to 30 my husband and I got in the car and drove through it and it was really pretty. Wow it is a great area. I don't know why my father or many people from my community never went there. They never even visited. Why? It was maybe a seven hour drive. Of course you start thinking about collective memory. Who knows why they never went. I started thinking about the American Revolution and why it separated us from this area and how historically we were driven from that land and ended up in Brantford along the Grand River because of that war, siding with the British and we were given this land along the Grand. I just thought was it the memory of that war that was passed on from one generation to the next generation that made people never want to return there even though they would talk about the place in dreamy ways. And then as they start getting older and meeting other people, even people my age, they started visiting this place too. People have an attachment there. People do want to visit and want to reconnect. I thought if we got enough people together they're going to say let's buy some land and start becoming part of this land again, but nothing like that has happened. But still people are still taken with that area and are visiting there.

From Six Nations they have these buses that follow the journey of the Peacemaker that take them into the area, that follow that story of Hiawatha and Peacemaker and trying to find those locations where certain things happened in that story. So having the Adirondacks in my work, I like including that in the work. I don't know if it is so much retelling that history, but for me it is to make that history real, and participating in something that my parents participated in, although for them it was a sort of second-hand kind of way, because by my father talking about this area but never going there, and just making me curious enough to go and see what the talk was about. I just find it really interesting, and then once people start going to that place it is almost like a nostalgia that comes into them. I don't know how to explain it, I don't think it's a romantic idea and it's not sentimental, it's something else – I don't know what the word is.

But there is a shift somewhere in your body when you go there, and you know about the history and you start thinking about where you are now, as opposed to where you were historically 250 years ago.

It's like a telepathy happening, but also very physical.

My father had never been there.

ML—That's remarkable. He was retransmitting what he had learned.

SN—Yes, putting it into me, and me going there, and then bringing back how it affected me and it's something that I never really paid too much attention to until I started going to these places. You see these places that happen in history books.

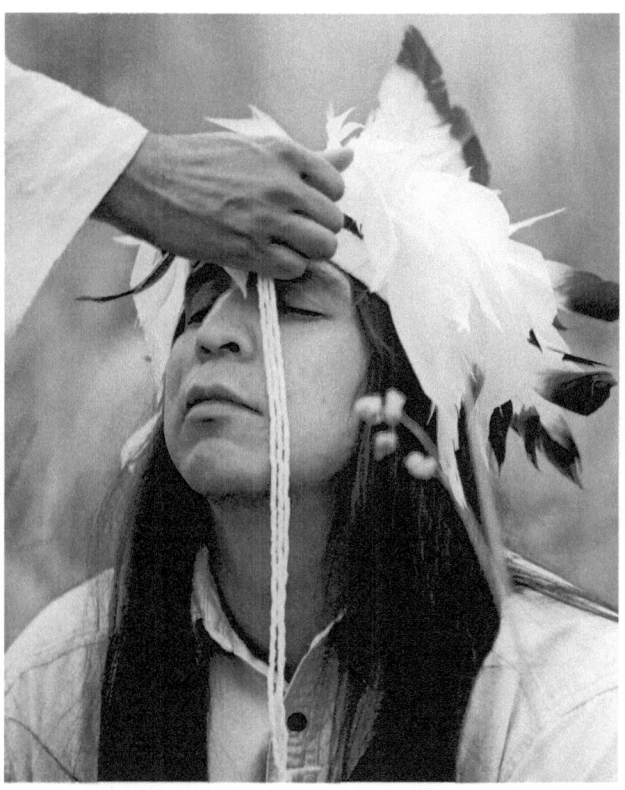

40. *Suite: INDIAN* [detail of film still]
    [Peacemaker and Hiawatha]
    2005

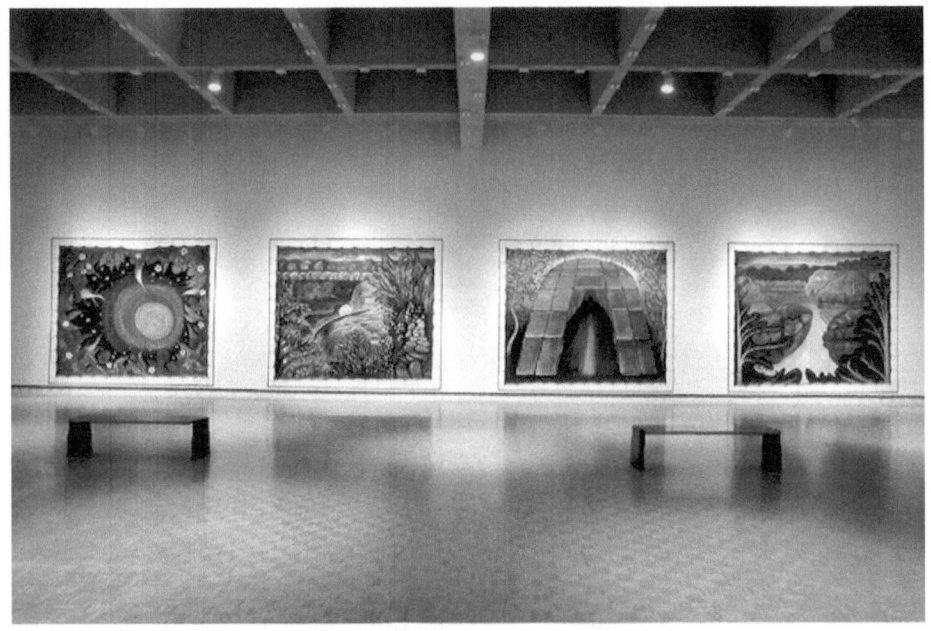

41. *Passage*
    installation photograph at Mendel Art Gallery, Saskatoon
    1996-97
    series of four oil paintings on canvas
    426.7 x 365.7 cm [each]

Once I went with my brother, it was his first time, though I had been a few times. He would start seeing the signage, like Cherry Valley – "THERE'S CHERRY VALLEY!" Which is quite amazing because these places are real and they're not that far away – he reacted like he had met some famous rock star! So he was – WOW. It's real!

ML – This idea of the bus tours to the Adirondacks tracing the Hiawatha myth is interesting. In your film [*Suite: INDIAN*] Hiawatha looks like he's on a beach on sand, he finds shells and he makes bead work – is the Adirondacks the location?

SN – In my film that's Lake Erie, but part of that story is that he is so totally depleted of everything because his family had been killed by his own people because they were jealous of his own power that he had this ability to make things happen. He became so depressed and almost catatonic that he couldn't do anything. He falls near this lake and he says if I am the great prophet then make the birds come and fly and take the water away. And they did. And he still can't come out of it because it doesn't mean any thing to him. That is when the Peacemaker finds him and sees he needs help. He takes the wampum beads and touches Hiawatha's head and little by little he comes out of it.

ML – How does this figure in your work? The paintings in *Passage* (1996-97) – is this the Adirondacks?

SN – *Passage* is a four painting series. The first one is the Sky Woman story, the creation story. I thought it was important to put it in there. It is the universal beginning of our history. And then we shift to the Cohoes where the Mohawk River meets the Hudson River, and in fact was the place where Peacemaker's challenged by Mohawks, saying we've had many prophets come this way before and they all said they could do wonderful things but they couldn't, so we don't believe you. Then he said, well tie me to this tree and throw it into the Falls. If I survive you can listen to what I have to say, and if I don't survive of course you don't have to listen to anything I say. They did, and he does survive and at that point people start listening to him and coming to terms about their own existence and deciding that there's a better way to live. That begins the Iroquois Confederacy, the initial stage. The next one is the longhouse painting. I use a painting of the longhouse because to me it represents the place where people will come together and make decisions together and really try to communicate in that one-mindedness. I think even though we don't go to the longhouse now, at least I don't, I think there are other examples where people do try to come together in one-mindedness. It could be universities or art galleries or even movie theatres where people participate together in something.

The last one is Grand River. That is the journey of Six Nations people, how they left the Mohawk Valley and ended up in Brantford, or Six Nations, along the Grand River.

ML—You use the Grand River in other works.

SN—Yes. When I was growing up even in school you were told our land starts at the source and goes to the mouth of the Grand River. We get six miles on both sides of that river. But now we don't have six miles. I think it's six miles by six miles on one side. Some of that land comes into contestation – who owns it, how did you get the deed to that, and all those questions. The thing that happened in Caledonia – the people there say they are the ones who own it, they can't prove it, and there is no deed. It is very maddening because as time goes on those issues will always be there, from one generation to the next generation, people die off. People burn out. I think it is just going to be there forever. People stay on that land for years and years and who's to say how they got to live there.

I like to address those issues and I know that I won't be able to solve them or even pretend to steer it in a direction. But I think it is good to remember because as time goes on people forget. Do you remember Stony Point Reserve? My dad said that when the war started it was an Indian reserve. When the war started all the men went off to war, and during that time the government came in and moved everybody off and made it into an army base. They were told they could have it back when the war was over, but when the war was over they never did get it back. (I believe they later had the area returned to them.)

So it's not about being a trouble maker or anything, but it is saying this is what happened and this is how it happened. I don't think the government really cares. It is frustrating because I don't like to make my work about those kinds of political things, but sometimes it leaks out. If my mind has to go that way then I let it go. But I don't force it to go that way. It seems to end up there.

ML – What about the question of 'audience'? When you are making art is it for you, or for a viewer, or does the question even occur to you?

SN—When I first started making art I made it for my family. If I thought if anyone would understand this art it would be them. So I kept focused on who this was for even though they might never see it. It helped a lot because I could direct it into being a little bit quirky or sad or something strange and I felt okay because there was a direction in the work. Now that I'm older it's not that I don't think about the audience as much, but I think that I do it for me now. It has to have a certain amount of depth in the work before I am happy with it, and only I can know the depth of the work. Not that I've gotten smarter than my sisters or my brother, but now if I directed it toward them I would feel that the depth wouldn't be there.

I think too, that before, when I was starting to make art I was looking in an abstract way for permission. Not that they would say oh yes you can do that, but it almost had to cross a certain boundary before I could be happy with making it. Whereas now I really am not aware of the boundaries. Having their presence somewhere in the work was helpful but now I don't need it.

ML—It must be interesting to look back on your work from this point in your career.

SN—A couple of years ago I went to my studio and threw out so much. Some of it I did keep – work that is kind of on the naïve side. But sometimes I come across something that is earlier and I think: well, that's not so bad, not as bad as I remembered.

In Hamilton a month ago, watching *Honey Moccasin*, it was really hard. I hadn't seen it in a long, long time. To see it again opened so many paths and

Conversation with Shelley Niro

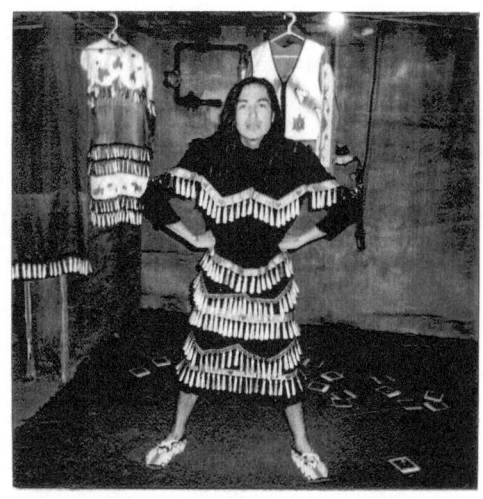

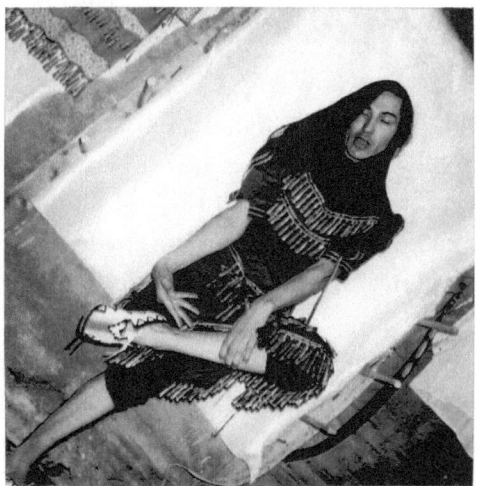

42. *Honey Moccasin* [film still]
    1998
    16 mm film, colour
    50 minutes

memories of making the work – everything came through my brain all at the same time: when I made it, why I made it, what was going on around me as I'm making it. It just seemed like everything rushed in. I should have looked at it before the screening. Steven [Loft] was asking me questions and I couldn't articulate what I was thinking about making this film. Sometimes it gets a little bit hard. You make something, put it away, and bring it back out and it blows up in your face.

When I started writing *Honey Moccasin* – well, I don't consider myself as a writer. It is hard for me to think of the words and sentence structure, but when I am writing a script, the ideas start percolating and bubbling away. And sometimes things come up, ideas that I wouldn't have suspected. The character of Zachary John – the guy who ends up being our cross dresser, powwow Jingle Dress dancer – jumped out and I thought 'Oh, that's different'. I sent the script to a couple of people, a couple of gay friends. I thought if they're offended by it I'll just put it away. But they were really excited about the character that I had created in *Honey Moccasin*. They said they'd never seen anything like it before. They were happy with the fact that Zachary John tells the bartender, Beau, 'I love you' and they had never seen that before so it was encouraging to hear that. I was really interested in creating something that was non-traditional and non-stereotypical and that was just different. But now when I look at it, it looks really dated! But it's fun.

ML—How did you get the money to make the film?

SN—The whole budget was seventy thousand. I had money from Canadian Heritage, from Canada Council for the

Arts, Ontario Arts Council – little bits and chunks of money here and there.

ML—The night at the Hamilton Art Gallery, looking at your films, it was interesting to see the shifts in your approach. The themes continue in different forms.

SN—That is important especially in film – they can sound the same. It is fun to see. Every time I've done something like that there is a different kind of camera, different kind of hardware, so you have to change in thinking how you are going to get it done.

ML—So the different technologies have an influence?

SN—Yes. *Kissed by Lightning* was done digitally. Everything can be done so fast. We didn't have time to rehearse. Everyone is so used to getting the camera, getting it set up, getting the actors set up. With film it feels like you are always sitting around waiting for everything to be set up. Whereas with digital it is: okay hurry up. It is a big issue.

You learn every time, with each project, especially being with different people.

Robert's Paintings started out with Robert Houle asking me to do a film on him, because he was affected emotionally by *Kissed by Lightning*. How can I say no to someone asking me to do this? He wanted to talk about his residential school experience. I thought this was a great opportunity because in my next film I have one of the parents of the main character who is a residential school survivor. I thought maybe I can get more insight into that character.

It took about a year and a half. We started in Paris,

because he was having a show at the Canadian Cultural Centre in Paris, and I thought that would be a great ending to the film. This artist who has gone through this turmoil in his life is now being shown in Paris at the Cultural Centre. We went there, filmed Paris, and filmed him at his show. And when we got back we started at the end of September – we went to Montreal, Ottawa, Toronto and Winnipeg and interviewed people he knew, interviewed some of his family, old friends, Alanis Obomsawin was one of them. She is such an historian in her own right about what Indian people in the country had to go through. She serves as a witness to the contemporary history of Native people in Canada. And of course we talked with his friend George Miller. We went to Winnipeg where his family was, talking to his sister, and filming at the Winnipeg pow wow. To me it's like the great synopsis of our history. So many other films that talk about the residential school system are heartbreaking and sad. I wanted Robert to show his work and talk about his own life. I wanted *Robert's Paintings* to be positive and forward moving. I thought it turned out beautifully.

ML—The way you had shots of him painting – the bed in the residential school, and then shots of the place with him talking about it, made it all real and you could understand how a child would be affected by it. I remember him describing being on the roof of the school building and seeing his house and knowing he could not go there. It is moving and unforgettable.

SN—I really like how the little boy is in there. He's my nephew. Just having that closure I thought was really important.

The film was shown at the *ImagiNative* festival in Toronto. Many people were affected and talked with Robert about it. They talked about how it helped them understand their parents who could not talk about anything. They are damaged, without any ability to show affection or anything. So it helps them be closer to their parents. I'm glad I did it.

ML—It's significant that Robert saw in you and your work the possibility to tell his story. Now you are working on another film?

SN—Yes. Now I am working on a feature length script. It's a narrative; it's fictional and has a fantasy element to it, which I really love. But fantasy is a hard thing to do because you can over-fantasize. It is called *The Incredible 25th Year of Mitzi Bearclaw*. She is living in Toronto and wants to be a fashion designer. Right now she is working at the Indian Centre and she is the street liaison person giving out soup and coffee at night. She has a boyfriend and his name is Ringo Leaves-No-Shadow. He's this handsome man and she is this crazy fashion girl. She also has a cousin who is a year younger who has lived with her family all his life because his parents have died. Her father writes to her and says please come home and help me look after your mother. She is a diabetic and it is the sad story of diabetics, she's blind and she can't walk anymore and he needs her to come home and help. She is angry, saying she doesn't like her mother, she's always been a bitch, but she'll go home because of her father. So she has to leave her sexy little life in Toronto and go back to the Northern Reserve. Once she gets there she is reacquainted with a trio of spiritual collaborators. The spirits are Hope, Faith and Charity. She slips into being depressed and they say "come on let's do something". They take her in a space ship and they go into outer space and they can see earth below – that sort of thing. It is all about being some place where you don't want to be, and where the possibilities are really limited, and about using your imagination to your best ability. It is about making that very limited environment as rich as you can. It's that kind of story.

Every year, I don't know if you read the papers but it seems to come in floods or in waves talking about suicides on reserves. That's where their story stems from. It's about creating a space for those kids that live in places that have absolutely no hope.

ML—You always pick the most challenging things – it is not the easiest subject to take up.

SN—Yes but I didn't want to do anything in such a literal way. I think about my own childhood living on the reserve where we were very poor, very limited, and didn't really realize how limited or how poor we were, but when we'd see something on TV that spoke to us – it was pretty amazing having that kind of stimulus.

ML—When you talk about your childhood, it sounds relatively happy. Your parents sound like caring, loving people. It doesn't sound horrific, whereas sometimes stories you hear sound awful, and you wonder how any human being can survive.

SN—It again comes down to the media. What are they benefiting from and who is steering in that direction? Just before Christmas stories about Attawapiskat started showing up. With those kinds of stories come the others, filling in as many crappy stories as they can. It would be different if something positive happened but they never cover the positive things. There was one story on the television on aboriginal youth in Winnipeg who started a soup kitchen for homeless people. I thought that was such a great story, but I never saw any thing else on it. No one picked it up.

ML—When you work on a film do you continue with work in other media?

SN—Yes because film is so expensive and it takes so long to get it made, from point A to point Z, and for me to make a 'thing' is so satisfying. If I can just make one thing and then another one, I am really happy. But film is so much fun. There are people who only make film and I wonder how they manage to stay creative. But it is so frustrating because the money is so slow.

ML—You work in different media. Are there certain messages that you want to communicate, or ideas you want to experiment with that suit some media more than others. For example, with the four *Passage* paintings you have also done similar photographs. Do you ever use photographs as tests for paintings or are they always separate works.

SN—I like to think of them as separate work. I find when I am painting I use one part of my brain and going to photography I find the whole thing has to shift. You've heard the expression 'dumb painters'? When I'm painting I'm really dumb – the whole day will go. I'll start at 9 and finish at 9 and I think wow where did the time go? Whereas with photography, everything has to be calculated – the size of the work, how am I going to frame it, how to mat it – everything is mechanical – that kind of thinking. With painting something happens to me. Now that I am using digital cameras – you are sitting in front of a computer pushing keys. You might have an art piece at the end of it all but you still have to know what the numbers mean. So it's different – a real different way of making stuff. Your brain has to work in a much different way.

ML—Those are major areas, painting, photography, film; but you also work in other areas. Now you are doing basket weaving, bead work, and sometimes in connection with something else.

SN—Beadwork is about rhythm, about technique and a certain kind of tension to keep the beads on the string and get them on the material. You have to have a specific idea of how you want it to end up. Whereas painting, photography – you kind of have to have an idea of how you'd like it to end up, but bead work you have to pin point ahead what you want to do with colours, the size of the beads. It has to have some kind of culturally significant look to it too, or else why do bead work. So it's a different way of thinking too.

ML—You have talked about the fact that some of the designs look like a cross and some things people mistake for Christian iconography. There is the story of a woman who conceives on her own and I remember saying to you, 'what, another Immaculate Conception?' That got me thinking about the need that humans have to find reasoning in the world around us, and how

we make sense of it. There are parallels in the belief
patterns in almost every culture. Some of them are
religious, some of them aren't. I think this is why I've
asked you questions: what is this, what does it mean,
what does this represent. Sometimes you think you
recognize something and then it's not what you think.
That's okay in terms of me as an individual in front
of an art work – I can make of it what I want. You
put your work out there and what people make of it is
up to them. On the other hand, it seems to me that in
knowing more about what's going on in your work, you
see more, you understand more, and it has much greater
meaning and significance for you as a viewer. I think it
must be difficult for an artist – how much information
can you convey? You convey what you know in ways
that make sense to you. Do you ever find it frustrating
when people like me come along and say 'what is this?'

SN—I don't try to hide stuff. But I want to make it
interesting enough so that when people look at it they
might be intrigued about the work, they will go and
seek out information about what's going on or what
the symbol means or something like that. I find that it
has to be interesting even if people don't know what's
going on in the work they are compelled to look at it
longer. Sometimes when you see a literal work in front
of you I think – does it have to be so literal? You don't
have to do that. Not that I try to insert iconography
into the work so that only a certain people understand.
I love it when I can look at other work from different
cultures and if I don't understand it then I want to
know what's going on. If you are so inclined to become
interested or excited by something it is worth passing
over that area, even if you don't get it or find out what

it was you are jumping a little bit. That happens to me a lot. I use music as the way of doing that. I can listen to something and think that it's really great. I don't know anything about the culture but there is just something that will make me become very curious about the work.

ML—You use music effectively in your film work.

SN—I love music. It is an art form that is beyond my comprehension. To be a musician or a composer you have to be so talented. Not everybody can compose. I really like using it.
    The musician/composer, Elizabeth Hill, for *Kissed by Lightning* – she is divinely inspired. She just goes into the studio ... For example in the last scene, everyone is standing around the fire; the woman and boy looking out at the window. There is a four-part harmony. I said to Elizabeth I need a little bit of four-part harmony right at the end and it has to sound like angels. And she did it in five minutes! It was magic and outstanding. That's pretty good! If it was me it would take me forever. So I think musicians and composers are angels. I am in awe of their wonderful work. I never get tired of that talent.

ML—There is one film you did from 2003, *The Shirt*. It is quite something. What kind of reaction do you get to that?

SN—That video got a great reaction. It was shown at the Sundance Film Festival in 2004 and at the Venice Biennale as part of the '50 extras'. It's been shown quite a bit. Someone came up to me once and said I saw your film in Russia, and I said, wow, great!

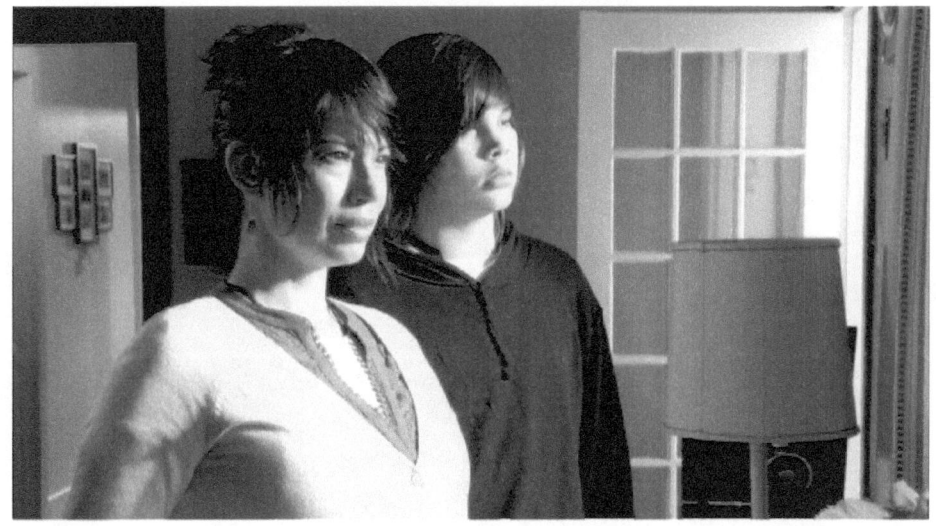

43. *Kissed by Lightning* [film still]
    2009
    HD video, colour
    90 minutes

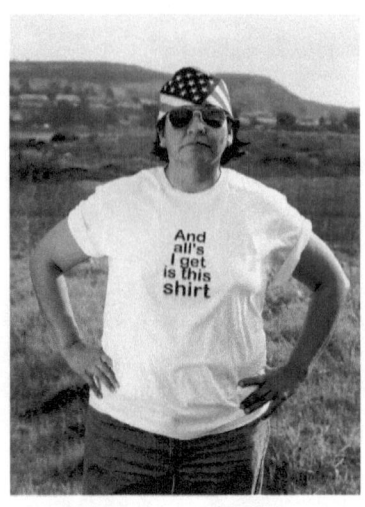

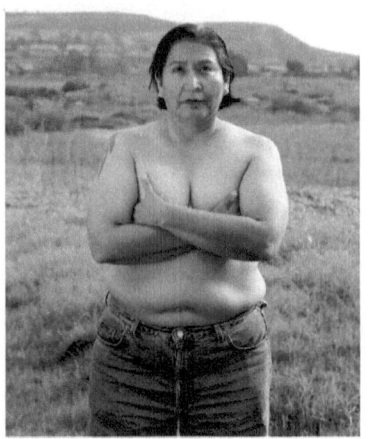

44. *The Shirt* [#6 and #7]
    2003
    series of 9 duratran prints in light boxes
    110 x 138 x 12 cm [each]

I have Hulleah Tsinhnahjinnie and her partner Veronica Passalacqua – they are the two characters in the film. I needed somebody who is really strong and Hulleah fits that role so well. I talked with her about it a year before I shot it. I told her 'I have this idea and I want to come [to California] and video tape you, can you do it?' And she said 'Yeah', Okay. I went there with my camera and shot her. In one of the scenes she takes her shirt off because she loses her shirt basically. I also did a photo installation of the work – there are 9 panels and they are on light boxes and are about 40 x 60 inches and I showed that quite a few places. We laugh because when we were doing it I said okay now I need you to take your shirt off and she was a good sport and did it. And then the video started going all over the place and she got all kinds of comments from people that she knew, and she said I didn't know it was going to go all over the world! Well, now we know!

ML — Why do you think it is so popular?

SN — The T Shirt has all these texts on it – my ancestors were massacred and exterminated and it's right-in-your-face comments, so it's really kind of out there but the bottom line is 'all I get is this shirt'. Being a native person in North America, all these horrible, horrible things happen and then as benefits for the loss of land, language and heritage, you might get dental care, you might get health care, you might get these sorts of things but as time goes on little bit by little bit they're taken away too. And then you get the new-agers who really want to suck up the culture and become the gurus of native spiritually. So I use the non-Native component to say now I'm wearing the shirt. The history of the native person is that we have this really horrible history in the US and in Canada, though it's more the US because of the headband she wears. And "All's I get is this shirt!"

ML—In the film you pan away over a landscape and then back to the figure.

SN—I wanted it to resemble the West. But now they tell me you wouldn't recognize that landscape – it is full of subdivisions and that happened a year or two after I shot it.

The idea just came to me. I was in a plane going over Texas and you could see all the land chopped up into parcels. I thought this is kind of sad. Everything is accounted for and commodified. Something has possession of this land. And that is when I started thinking of this video project. They were massacred and exterminated and everything is chopped up.

ML—It is a very accessible work, very clear and humorous. We haven't talked about your sense of humour. I think that blesses your work. It makes it possible for people to take in some very difficult messages and makes the work human. You are an individual, these are stories, it is history, it is contemporary life (and if you don't laugh you might cry). It is there in your early work – it is your personality. Take *Mohawks in Beehives* (1991) and those photos – you are having fun but the message is serious. And when people can laugh they can accept more.

SN—Humour is a funny thing. You can't plan the humour: you can't say 'I'm going to make a funny thing.' The

Conversation with Shelley Niro

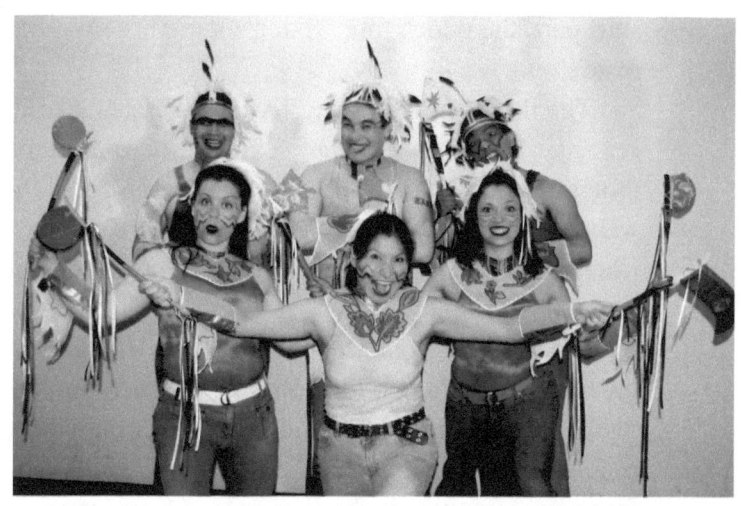

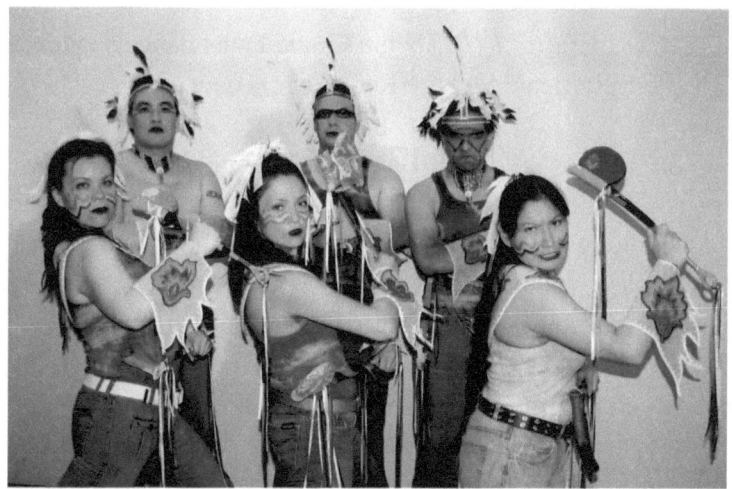

45. *Suite: INDIAN* [film stills]
    [dance of the canoe pants sequence, Dancers: Garret Jones, Niso
    Shawanda, Sid Bobb, Nanta Hill, Kristol Abel, Santee Smith]
    2005
    photographs courtesy of Brenda Mitten

shirt part, the punch line – I don't know where it comes from.

The thing about humour [Allan J. Ryan's *The Trickster Shift*] – people only expect you to do funny things after a while. I kind of resent that because they want to label you and it becomes this weird thing where they will only accept it if it's funny. So it is a tricky thing to play.

In *Kissed by Lightning* the character Bug had the funny parts in that film. He was the buffoon, the one in the telephone booth falling all over the place, accidentally hurting himself all the time. He played that part. And there is the character of Sun-June in the gallery – he's kind of funny too ... the art world.

ML—In *Suite: INDIAN* the Canoe Pants dance sequence is hysterical. And the Red Army sequence too.

SN—I showed that at Hamilton College in New York. Someone in the audience was devastated that I used a song from the Red Army Orchestra and Choir. "Why are you using that song? We had to march to that every morning!" I didn't know it was going to effect you that way, sorry! It is such a great song and the title is "The Red Army is the Strongest," so how appropriate.

The history of the Red Army Orchestra and Choir is that they were used for propaganda, sent off by the Tsar to play for the army when the men had no coats, ammunition or food, to encourage them to fight. Horrible. The Russians always have such great music and horror stories.

ML—We always return to film, and yet your photography is also stunning in many ways.

SN — Photography is a medium you see everywhere and so there is a certain expectation of the perfection of photography. I find that to use photography especially the way I use it you have to invent a different world all the time, using the camera. I have to think about what I haven't seen that I can show because it is so easy to fall back into what's acceptable. It is like drawing for me because it is a challenge. You have to spin your wheels and think about making something original and meaningful, and hopefully it's beautiful.

ML — There are installations that have a number of photographs like *Surrender Nothing Always* that are very powerful.

SN — That piece is 12 feet long. *Surrender Nothing Always* – in one hand he has the turtle rattle and in the other hand brushes and a palette knife. It's about using your brain and your memory in trying to create something so that it speaks to your community, and not surrendering.

There is the series *Borders-TREATIES* (2008), with only the hands and arms depicted. There are four photographs. The first is the man and the woman reaching out to each other, called *Boundless*. On the bottom of that one there is the DNA string, on the top there are birds and the last is an airplane. It speaks about evolution and how things evolve and change. Basically society is made up of people who want to look after each other but that have to be in pursuit of the inevitable and what is changing before anybody else, because if you don't change before other people, you're gone. The second one is *Borders*, two male hands, fists, coming together and the bottom shows fences and the top row is a row of barbed wire. The third one is *Treaties*. It is

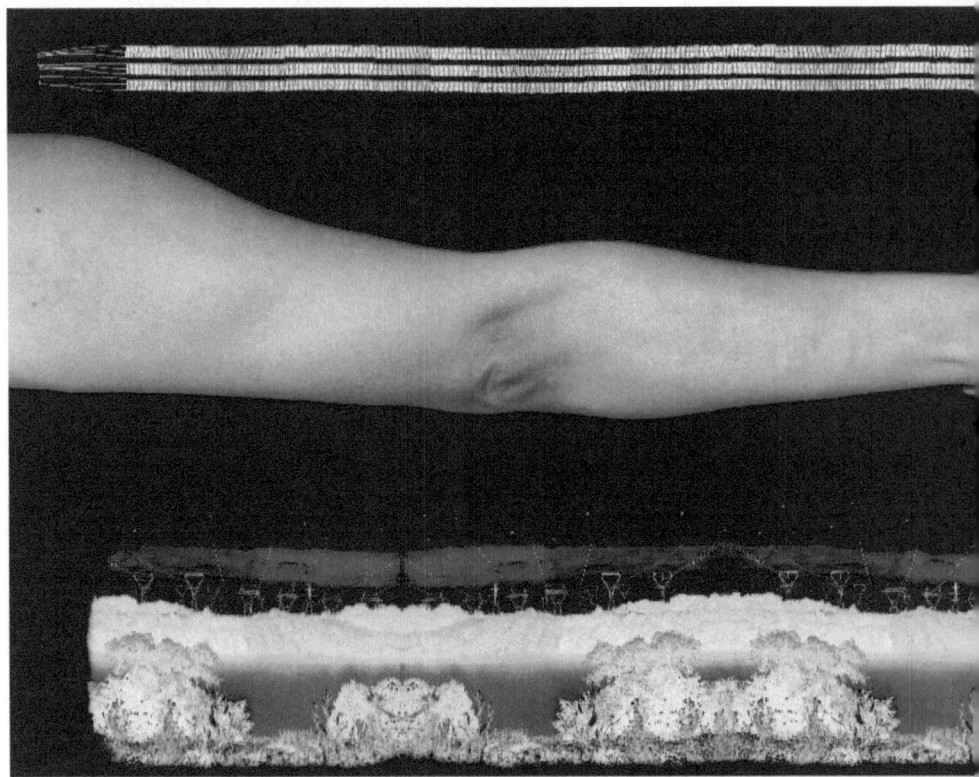

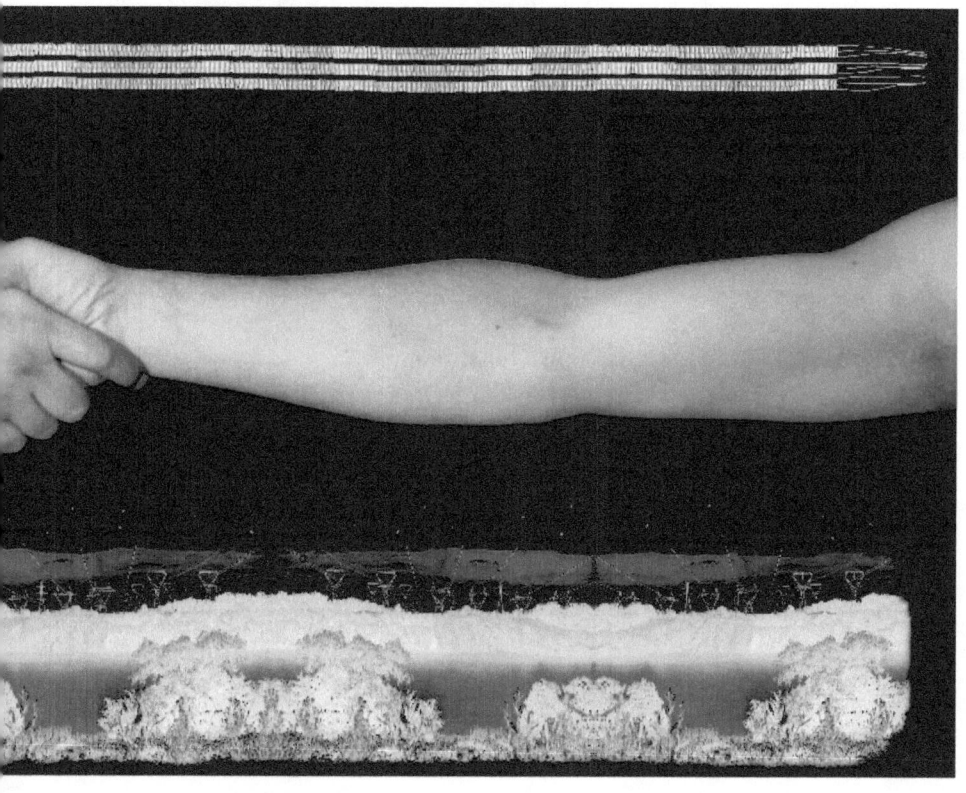

46. *Treaties*
    from the series *Borders-TREATIES*
    2008
    digital photograph
    122 x 45 cm

two hands coming together again but it is a handshake. The bottom row in *Treaties* is the river and it's lined with trees and with hydro towers. The top row is the two-row wampum. The fourth one is called *Unity* and the arms are gripping each other. The bottom row is images of an elder, a young woman, a young girl, a dog, and stars in a constellation. The top is twigs tied together to show unity, so everything is connected.

ML—Another installation *Unbury my Heart* (2000-2001) is very moving.

SN—There are four paintings: *Water*, *Fire*, *Land* and *Air*. It was made around the same time when fishing rights, land rights and all kinds of issues were circulating. When I started painting that series I was in New Mexico, and there was a big fire that went on for weeks. I was sitting outside with a friend and all these ashes are coming down. I was thinking about the forest, who knows how long it's been there and now it's just ashes that are flying around ... thinking about things that have been here a long time and then are gone in a poof of ash. There is a water scene and it speaks to fishing rights and how native people are only allowed to fish two cod a year or something like that. So these things were going through my mind at the time. And then I started thinking about *Bury My Heart at Wounded Knee*, but I thought I don't really want to bury I want to unbury, so it became *Unbury My Heart*. I made 500 velvet hearts and stuffed them and sewed them all together on these long ropes that were dyed different colours and spread them out in front of the paintings. It bothers me that so many times these issues are brought out by people who don't know the

Conversation with Shelley Niro 121

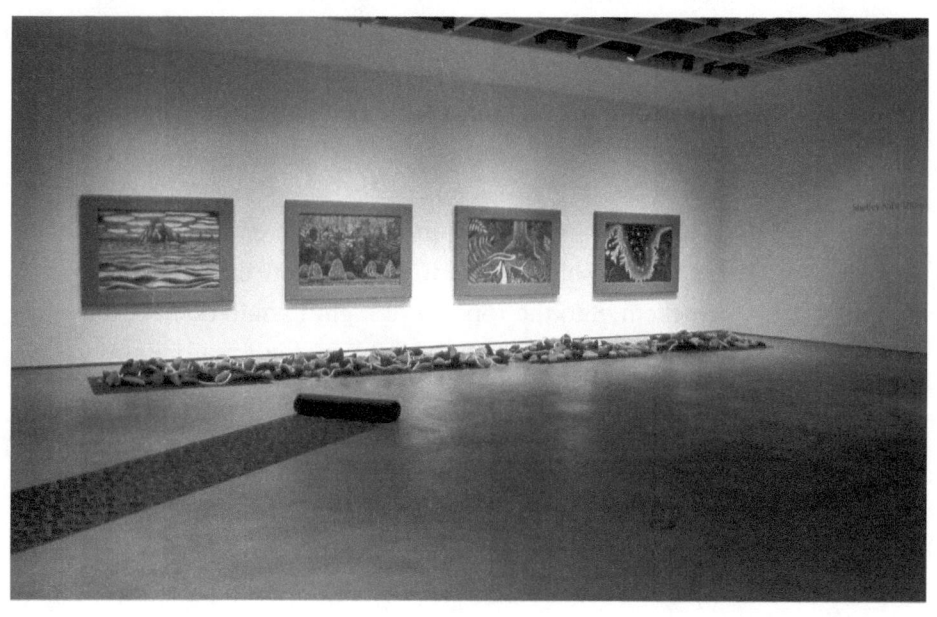

47. *Unbury My Heart*
 installation photograph at McMaster Museum of Art, Hamilton
 2000-2001
 series of four oil paintings (*Water, Fire, Land, Air*)
 152.4 x 91.4 cm [each]
 [with four carpets and 500 velvet hearts with 12 dyed nylon ropes]

real issue who say Native people are robbing from the taxpayer. It becomes this mantra where people want to blame Native people for these dumb things. We are really invested in this land, and I like to think that even though we are sort of lost in that spiral of legality at the moment there is more to it than that. That's where this piece came from.

ML—It is complex and must have been time-consuming to make.

SN—It was really time-consuming. By the end of making that I had to hire people to help to stuff the hearts and sew them onto the ropes. I thought I could do 500, ten a night, for how many nights? You don't really know how much 500 is until you start.

ML—It's described as having four carpets. What are they about?

SN—I put the four carpets one in front of each painting. They are red to symbolize – not a river – but I wanted it to feel like there is passion there. This was shown at the McMaster Museum and then went to the Eiteljorg Museum in Indianapolis and the Eiteljorg now owns it.

ML—You had a fellowship at the Eiteljorg.

SN—Yes it was great. It was their second year. They give a chunk of money and they buy a piece of work from you. It was amazing, a really great time. They bring you there to Indianapolis. They choose five artists every other year. I knew some of them but met others for the first time.

I have gone to Banff, too. I painted *Passing Through* (1993) at Banff. I developed photographs there that are 4 x 6 feet and I did the five paintings there in a studio. I was there for six weeks. It was good to be with a lot of other artists.

ML—There is also an appealing painting called *Losing My Stuff* from 2002.

SN—That's one of the titles from the Sky Woman series. The first is *Getting Ready for the Fall*, the next is *Losing My Stuff*, then *Dreaming*, and the last is *Loving It*.

ML—Do you think of any of these as self-portraits?

SN—No.

ML—You have done some portraits but not many – *This Land is Mime Land* is one example.

SN—There is one called *Waitress* – a painting of me as a waitress, a skinny waitress. I have done a few self-portraits but not many. Sometimes I do it because I need someone in the work. *Waitress* is a painting from 1985. I am a waitress and there is a customer, and I am accidentally spilling wine on the customer. Brian Mulroney and Mila are in the background dancing away. I did that after there was a First Ministers conference with Brian Mulroney and he had all these First Nations people there. He talked to them looking like he had a smirk on his face the whole time. I thought how disrespectful he looks with these people, talking about housing and getting better water, having all these things that are necessary for a better life.

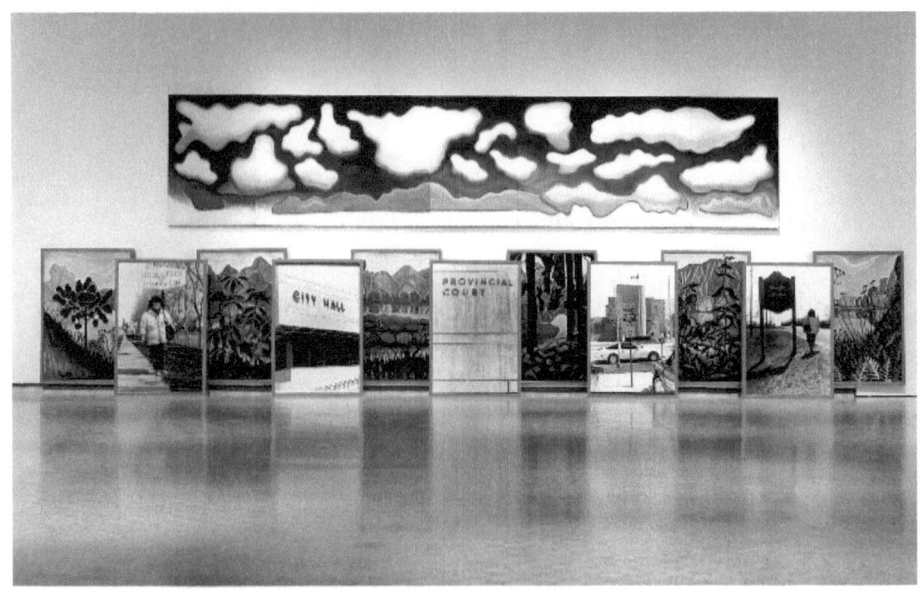

48. *Passing Through*
 installation photograph at London Regional Art
 and Historical Museum
 1993
 series of oil painting and photographs
 12.5 x 5.8 m [total size]

He looked like he was not paying attention, or did not really care. That is where this painting *Waitress* came from. I am standing on a floor with beadwork designs on it and there are burning False Faces in the background, so it is an angry painting.

When I was trying to figure out *M: Stories of Women*, I was in the planning stage. I didn't know if it would be a self-portrait series and I produced *The Moon and Me and a Celestial Tree* (2010).

ML—What is your process – does it often happen that you will use a work as you plan?

SN—Yes, when I am trying to work through it. *The Moon and Me and a Celestial Tree* – it was too much fun for me. So I thought I have to go deeper with this project. It cannot be so playful. It needs other layers in there. It was something I wanted to think about.

I always start off with something that I can throw away. I know I won't be using it but you have to start somewhere.

ML—*M: Stories of Women* includes very powerful images. What did you want to communicate?

SN—I am interested in getting images of women so that other people can see them. Native women are the poorest people in the continent of North America. Many times people don't want to take that seriously. It becomes easy to dismiss them. With this exhibition I want them to see women. These women are looking right out at you.

Bagging It – that's me. I didn't want to challenge the viewer, but I wanted the works to confront the viewer:

"You have to look at me and realize that I'm here."

The objects in this are body bags. Remember when there was the disaster – instead of sending the H1N1 antidote to the Northern Ontario Reserve, they sent body bags. That was just horrible. Even if it was a mistake – what was that about?

In this representation there is a bird in my ovary area and it is the cosmos and I see it as asteroids and energy coming out of my body. The sculpture represented is in downtown Brantford, part of the Joseph Brant monument. On each side there are plaques, about MEN. This one has a woman carrying a bowl of water. How typical, the men are standing around talking and the woman is carrying water for them. And I always put my dog Brandy in my work – there is supposed to be a dog in the Sky Woman story. I always weave bits of that story in.

Ancestor has an astronaut look, with constellations in the margin. I used buckskin for the cut-out frame in each work. Tanning the hide of buckskins was women's work so I took a couple of them and changed some of the shaping around it but I wanted them to be framed with that. *Memories of Flight* is a young woman with birds and wind turbines – I see these and hydro poles as signs of power, using up resources. They will take the land even if it's for this purpose.

Blanket – the Hudson Bay blanket and price coding bar and in the background are the four direction colours, it is laid on water. Water is commodified and taken and used. Even the history of Hudson Bay is so horrible for Native women. The woman represented here is a fantastic artist and she is very powerful.

Finding your Helpers is Sky Woman – the story is she is falling towards the water below her and as she

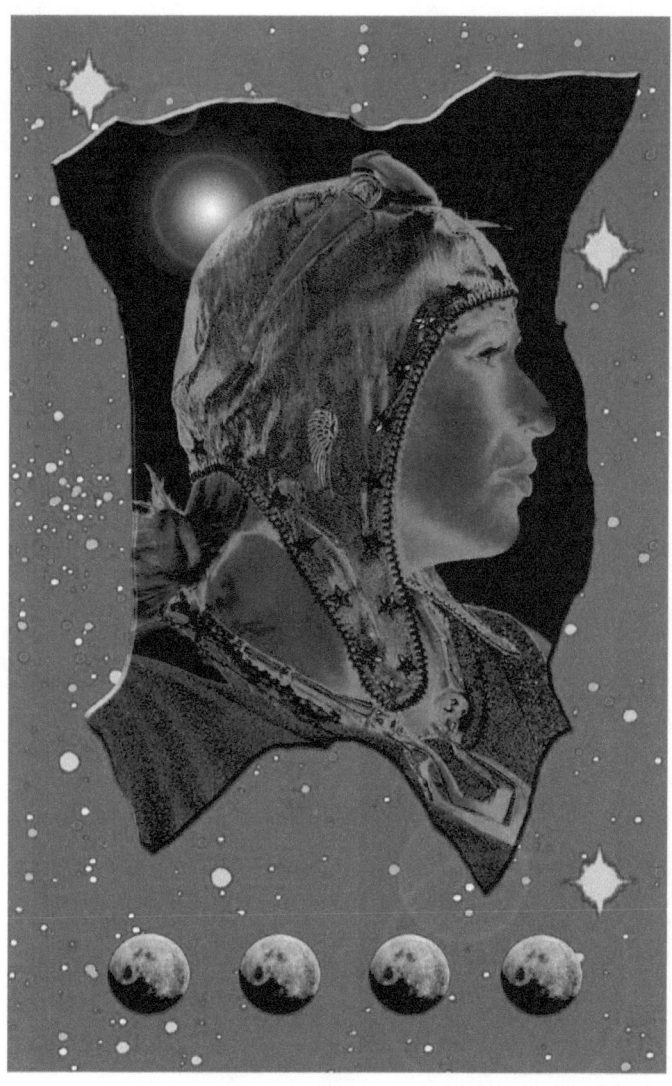

49. *Ancestor*
    from the series *M: Stories of Women*
    2011
    digital print
    101.6 x 152.4 cm

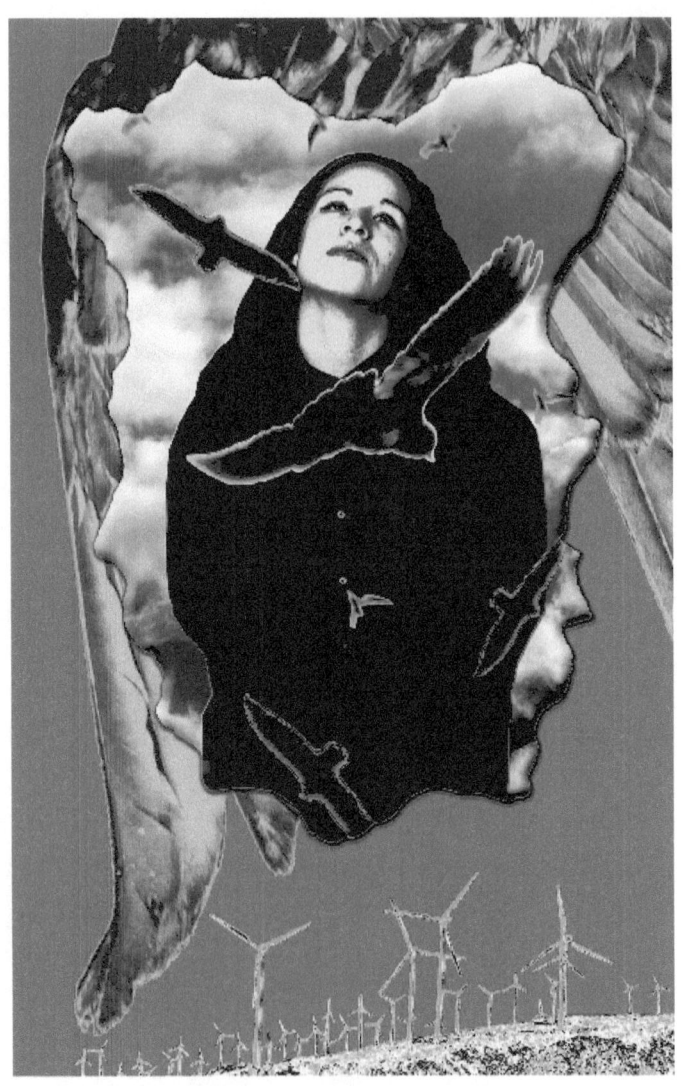

50. *Memories of Flight*
    from the series *M: Stories of Women*
    2011

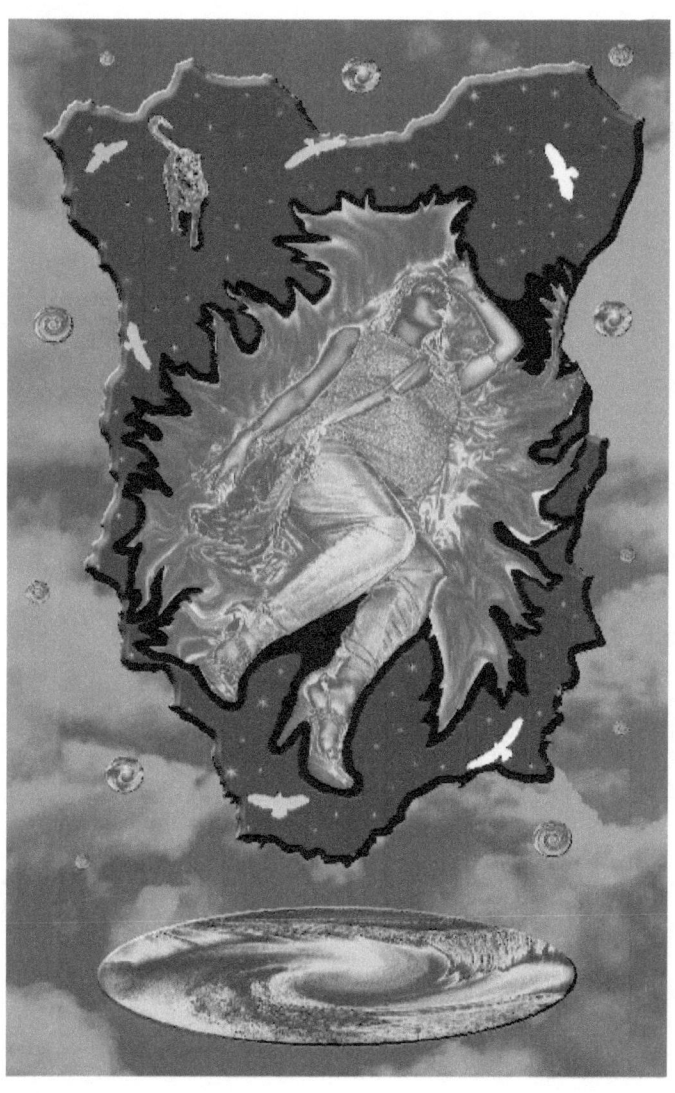

51. *Finding Her Helpers*
    from the series *M: Stories of Women*
    2011

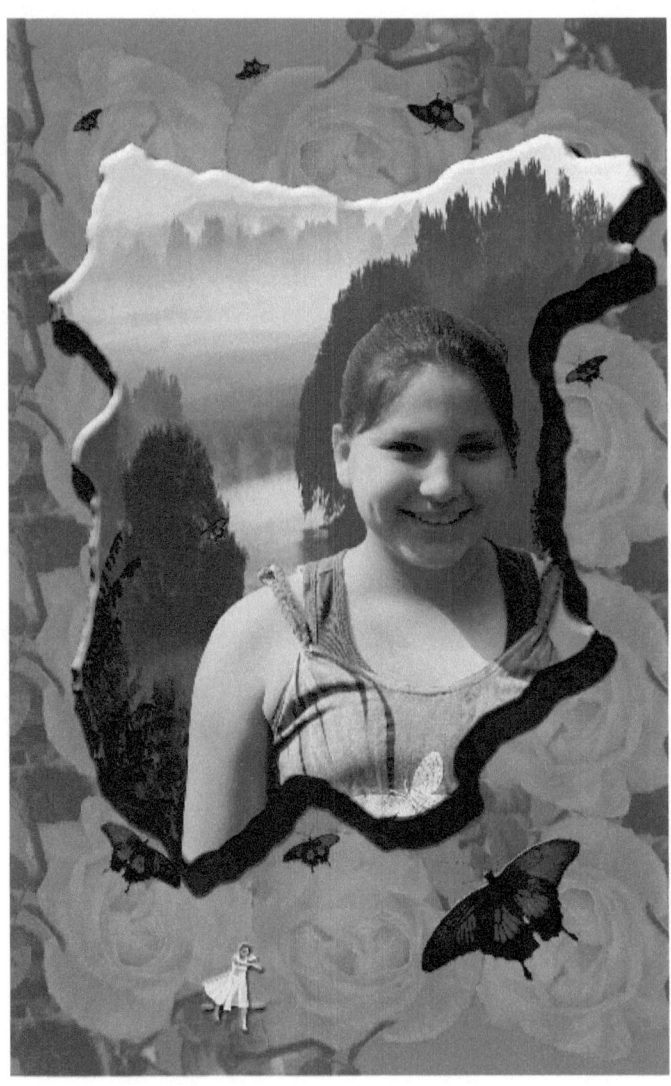

52. *Land of Opportunity*
from the series *M: Stories of Women*
2011

falls the animals are coming up out of the water saying: "What's going on, something's happening and we don't know what it is, we've never seen this before." They've had a council and they've decided it's a woman falling from the sky, and they decide to send something up to help her. They send all these birds that help her come down on the back of a turtle.

ML — Your woman is so powerful with her high-heeled boots and her jeans. She looks pregnant and there seems to be fire coming out of her mouth.

SN — In the Photoshop process shop you can solarize something in the photo to give it a glow, and here it is around her mouth. I wanted her to look like a space ship as she is going through the atmosphere.

ML — There are many parts to this series, but the most hopeful one is *The Land of Opportunity*. The girl has such a beautiful smile and behind her is a landscape with trees and a mist, and filled with butterflies. It is one of the most positive works in the face of all the rest. You found a way to bring optimism into it. This is part of much of your work. You have an optimistic side despite what could bring you down.

SN — You have to work at being optimistic. It is so easy to feel: why bother trying. It is something that keeps me interested in making art. You have to find it, discover it. If it is not showing up then I look for something else. I don't know how people can stop making art.

ML — Among the installations where you include photographs and other materials, there is one that

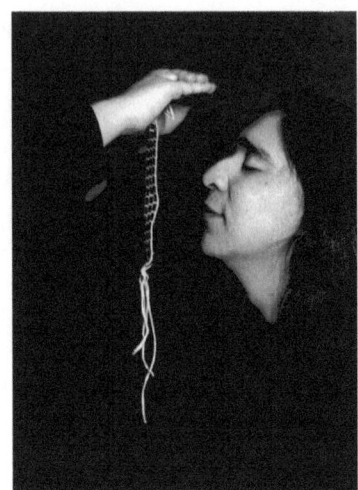

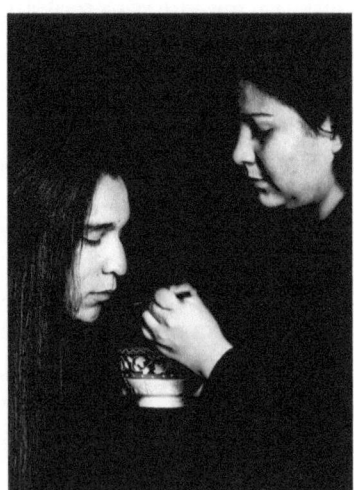

53. *The Essential Sensuality of Ceremony* [holding wampum and feeding]
    2002
    black and white photographs
    101.6 x 127 cm [each]

is very affecting, called *The Essential Sensuality of Ceremony* from 2002.

SN—That one comes back to the Peacemaker story. That story is told over a ten day period and is known as The Great Law. I wanted to know what was taking place in the story and what was The Great Law and what came out of it and why it was so important. I wanted the bottom line of the whole thing. So after reading a few versions of it I realized that it is all about awakening the senses. The whole story comes from a period of time when Native people's population went from 19 million to about 600,000. Some people say this happened after first contact when flu would sweep through the whole continent. The ones that remained, who survived, they lost all the social graces, they lost their elders, they lost ceremonies, basically forgot how to live together as a community. I don't know how long – centuries passed and people did not know how to get along as a community. There was a lot of warfare and horrible things going on. There had been a prophecy that a prophet would come into the territory and help people recover and make people's lives better. Finally he did show up, and was known as Peacemaker. A part of his story was to teach people what to eat. There was cannibalism happening so he would show people the correct things to eat. Also in the story there is always the burning of tobacco, the laying of hands, wiping away the tears of grief so you can think with a clear mind. There is always singing. So I interpreted those as things that are done to create stimulation in a person who is comatose or in a state of non-reaction.

There are five photographs. I used a man and a woman rather than man-man. The woman is feeding him, she's whispering in his ear, saying something to him. She is wiping away the tears from his eyes and holding wampum to his forehead. Each photograph demonstrates those elements that have to be brought into the ceremony to bring the person that represents the nation out of that catatonic state.

When I first showed the photographs I had in front of each photograph a small thing like little bells to jingle, or something to smell or touch to represent, to awaken the senses. On top I had little copper things that represented energy. I wanted to create this continuous energy between the object and the thing on top. I showed it like that a few times and then I thought that the photos really don't need that. If anything, these things are stopping the photo from being seen, so I took away those objects and now when it is shown, it is just the photographs themselves.

The interaction between the man and the woman is such a great dynamic between them.

This work has nothing around the frames but there is another series, *Ghosts, Girls and Grandmas* (2004), a series of five photographs. I beaded a frame piece and I used wampum beads, commercial wampum. I didn't want the wampum to represent anything specific. I wanted to make the photo look like it was surrounded with the energy of wampum. So it was free form wampum that doesn't do anything. Even talking about this work takes away some of the mystery in the photos, because I don't really know why I used some of those photos. The first one is of a man who looks like he is walking through the photograph, so you get a ghost feeling of the photograph in that work. The next one is a photograph of rocks on the ground. I think it is about being invested in the landscape, in

Conversation with Shelley Niro

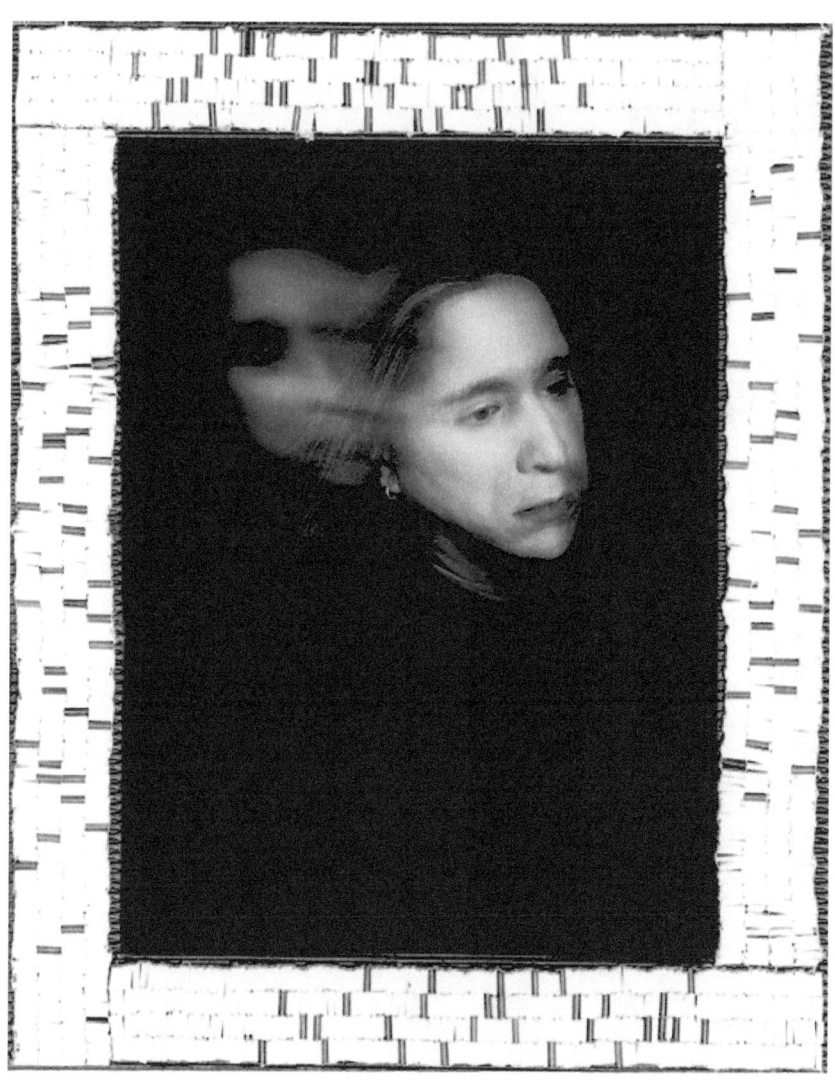

54. *Ghosts, Girls and Grandmas* [ghost]
    2004
    black and white photographs with wampum border
    76 x 101 cm

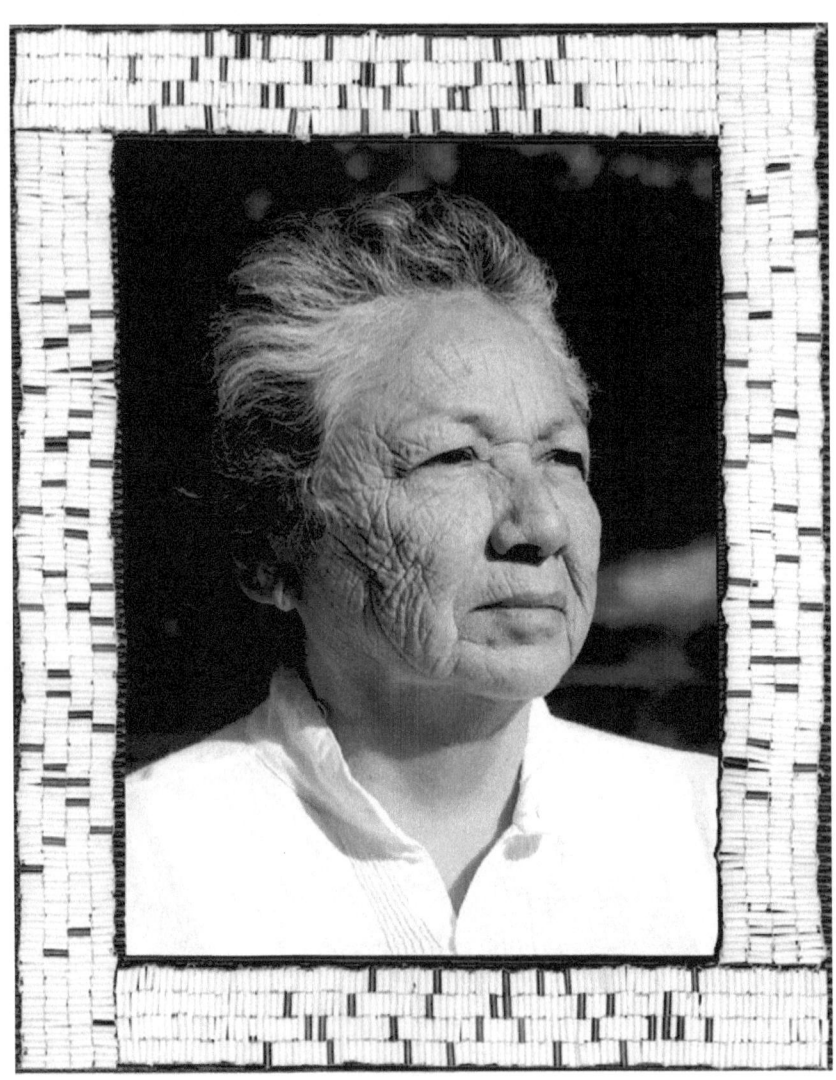

55. *Ghosts, Girls and Grandmas* [grandma]
2004
black and white photographs with wampum border
76 x 101 cm

Conversation with Shelley Niro

the environmental elements like when you are out in that atmosphere. The third one is a girl and her dog. The fourth is trees overhead and again it is the movement of the trees and the wind. The last one is the grandmother. For me those elements conjure up the ability for storytelling. Where do you get your stories from? If you're in nature it has to be the things that are around you, and the things you could take for granted but if you start paying attention to become really interested and it makes that environment so much more interesting as well.

Every time I try I can't really articulate what's happening with this work.

I like to think too that when you look at these things you can hear the wind, and when you see those rocks you are hearing things from the natural setting. If you allow yourself to pay attention to that setting it can stimulate something else that will take you to another place.

ML—Some of the same things are happening in your film *Tree* (2007). There seem to be vibrations in the atmosphere that show up as abstractions. The young woman stands on a stone by the water and things seem to happen around her, vibes around her, and she seems so alone within nature. The camera pans back and forth on the lake and she moves onto the shore. Then the camera stands behind her and we see a city in front of her. It is a powerful moment.

SN—I see it as Mother Nature arising. She (played by Lena Recollect) is coming out to see what's going on in the world. When she gets here she is not happy with what she sees. One of the images used in *Tree* is the dome

Madeline Lennon

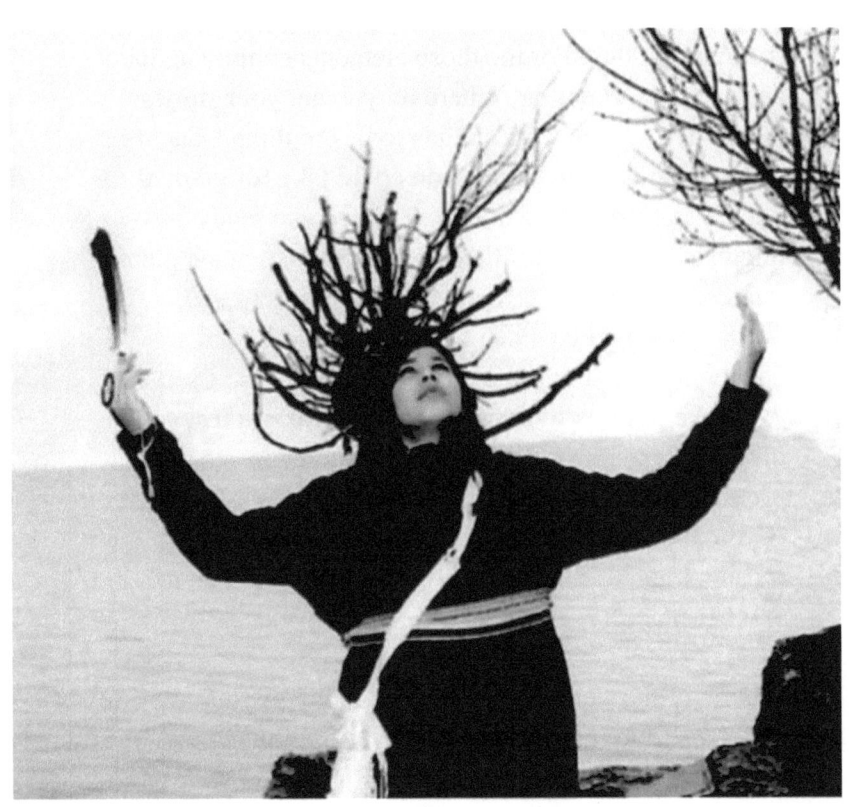

56. *TREE* [film still]
    2007
    mini DV, black and white
    5 minutes

Conversation with Shelley Niro

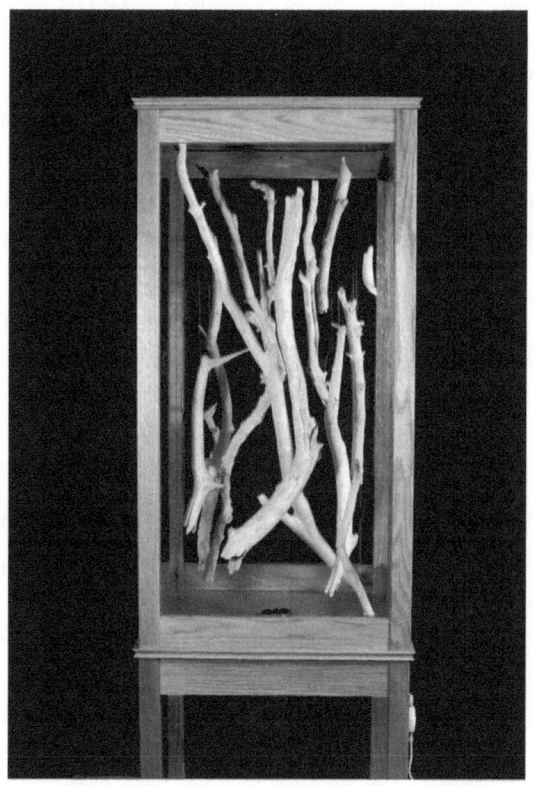

57. *Requiem for an 1812 Forest*
    2012
    wood sticks stained white and stones in cabinet
    dimensions variable
    image courtesy Niagara Art Centre, St. Catharines

from Hiroshima – you see the fire and things that have destroyed a part of the world. By destroying a part of the world you are really destroying the world. At the end of the film she is saddened by it, by the world as it is. We see the look on Recollect's face at the end when she looks up at the sky and sighs – the film is left open-ended. With all the destruction that happens in the world, it is a pretty sad little film.

Making the film I thought it is a sad little film – and I think: does the world need another sad film?

ML—There must be times when it is hard to avoid this kind of sadness. Recently you showed a new work *Requiem for an 1812 Forest* (2012) that seems to speak to human loss.

SN—I went to Queenston Heights, the site of a War of 1812 battle. I looked around and found sticks that had fallen from the trees on the site, brought them home and let them dry out. Then I carved out the dead parts and was left with a really hard wood – they are sticks of different shapes with nice twists and turns. I used white stain on them so that they suggest bones. The Niagara Arts Centre built upright cabinets and I arranged the sticks vertically inside, and then added light stones at the bottom. Native people fought in this war but this is too often forgotten.

ML—This year the Ontario Arts Council established a new award for Aboriginal Arts. You are its first recipient.

SN—Yes, it was the artist and and YOUME Gallery owner Bryce Kanbara who decided to nominate me for this award. I was honoured to be nominated, but then I didn't think about it because these things take time. At the end of May when I was informed that I had been chosen to receive it, I was so excited. It is fantastic!

I am not sure yet of exactly what establishing this award will mean, but we will see that over time. It is important to bring attention to Aboriginal art in Ontario. Hopefully one result will be that this art is taken more seriously. One of the best things about this award is that it allows the laureate to nominate an emerging Aboriginal artist, to bring more attention to that person's work. I chose Tracey Anthony because his art is impressive and deserves to be better known. I am honoured to have been chosen for this award by the Ontario Arts Council.

Bibliography

Abbot, Lawrence. "Interviews with Loretta Todd, Shelley Niro and Patricia Deadman," *Canadian Journal of Native Studies*, vol. 18, no. 2 (1998): 335-373.

Allen, Jan. *The Female Imaginary* [exhibition catalogue]. Kingston, Ontario: Queen's University, 1994.

Barkhouse, Mary Anne. "Truth and Dare: Profile on Shelley Niro," *Matriart*, vol. 3, no. 3 (1993): 4-6.

Beading, L.L. "In an 'Indian' Key: Shelley Niro's Revisioning of the Baroque Suite Form in Suite: INDIAN," in *Canadian Journal of Film Studies/Revue Canadienne d'Etudes Cinematographiques*, vol. 20, no. 2 (2011): 111-127.

Berlo, Janet C. and Ruth B. Philips. *Native North American Art. Oxford History of Art*. Oxford, New York: Oxford University Press, 1998.

Bigfeather, Joanna. *Native Views: Influences of Modern Culture* [exhibition catalogue]. Ann Arbor, MI: Artrain USA, 2004.

Corcoran, Sherry. *Shelley Niro: Outside the Columns* [exhibition catalogue]. Buffalo NY: UB Art Gallery, 2008.

Dowell, Kristin L. "Performance and 'Trickster Aesthetics' in the Work of Mohawk Filmmaker Shelley Niro," in S.E. Wilmer, *Native American Performance and Representation*. Tucson: University of Arizona Press, 2009.

Drouin-Brisebois, Josée, Greg A. Hill and Andrea Kunard. *It Is What It Is. Recent Acquisitions of New Canadian Art* [exhibition catalogue]. Ottawa: National Gallery of Canada, 2010.

Frater, Sally. *Shelley Niro: M: Stories of Women* [exhibition catalogue]. Toronto: Gallery 44, 2011.

Friesen, Andrea. *Speak for the Trees*. Seattle: Marquand Books, Inc., 2009.

Garneau, David. "Beyond the Pale: Looking for E/quality Outside the White Imaginary," in *Parallélogramme* vol. 20, no. 1 (1994): 34-43.

Harlan, Theresa. "Indigenous Photographies: A Space for Indigenous Realities," in Jane Alison, ed., *Native Nations: Journeys in American Photography*. London: Barbican Art Gallery, 1998, 233-245.

Heard Museum. *Watchful Eyes: Native American Woman Artists* [exhibition catalogue]. Phoenix, Arizona: The Heard Museum, 1994.

Henry, Victoria, and Shelley Niro. *From Icebergs to Iced Tea* [exhibition catalogue]. Thunder Bay and Ottawa: Thunder Bay Art Gallery and Carleton University Gallery, 1994.

Higginson, Catherine. "Shelley Niro, Haudenosaunee nationalism, and the continued contestation of the Brant monument," in *Essays on Canadian Writing*, no. 80 (December 2003): 141.

Hill, Lynne. *Alter Native: Contemporary Photo Compositions* [exhibition catalogue]. Kleinburg, Ontario: McMichael Canadian Art Collection, 1995.

Hill, Richard William, ed. *The World Upside Down: Le monde à l'envers* [exhibition catalogue]. Banff, Alberta: The Banff Centre Press, 2008.

Indyke, Dottie. "Shelley Niro," *Southwest Art*, vol. 34, no. 10 (March 2005): 42, 44.

Jurakic, Ivan and Steven Loft. *Shelley Niro: Almost Fallen* [exhibition catalogue]. Cambridge, Ontario: Cambridge Galleries, 2008.

Kalafatic, Carol. "Keepers of the Power: Story as Covenant in the Films of Loretta Todd, Shelley Niro, and Christine Welsh," in Kay Armatage, *Gendering the Nation: Canadian Women's Cinema*. Toronto: University of Toronto Press, 1999, 109-119.

Keating, Neal B. *Iroquois Art, Power, and History*. Norman: University of Oklahoma Press, 2012.

Keating, Neal B. *Native Perspectives / George Longfish / Shelley Niro* [exhibition catalogue]. Clinton NY: Emerson Gallery, Hamilton College, 2006.

Knapp, Millie. "Shelly Niro: Seductive Humor," in *Aboriginal Voices* vol. 3, no. 3 (July/August/ September 1996): 31.

Lippard, Lucy, et al. *LAND/ART*. New Mexico. Albuquerque N.M.: D.A.P., 2009.

Lorenz, Carol Ann. *Creation: Haudenosaunee Contemporary Art and Traditional Stories* [exhibition catalogue]. Cazenovia, NY: Stone Quarry Hill Art Park, 2004.

Miranda, Jose Mansilla. *Via Renovatur / North-South* [exhibition catalogue]. Ottawa: Le Groupe Agriculturel, Editors, 1994.

Mithlo, Nancy Marie, ed. *Manifestations. New Native Art Criticism*. Santa Fe, New Mexico: Museum of Contemporary Native Arts, 2011.

Mithlo, Nancy Marie. "Reappropriating Redskins: Pellerossasogna (Red Skin Dream): Shelley Niro at the 50th La Biennale di Venezia," in *Visual Anthropology Review*, vol. 20, no. 2 (September 2004): 22-35.

McMaster, Gerald. *Unbury My Heart* [exhibition catalogue]. Hamilton, Ontario: McMaster Museum of Art, 2001.

Neumaier, Diane, ed. *Reframings: New American Feminist Photographies*. Philadelphia: Temple University Press, 1995.

Nicholson, Heather Norris, ed. *Screening Culture: Constructing Image and Identity*. Lanham, Boulder, New York, Oxford: Lexington Books, 2003.

Niro, Shelley. *An Essential Personal Journey Through Iroquois Myths, Legends, Icons and History*. MFA Thesis, University of Western Ontario, London, Ontario, 1997.

Pearlstone, Zena. "Shelley Niro," in *American Indian Art Magazine*, vol. 36, no. 1 (Winter 2010): 61.

Phillips, Ruth B. *Trading Identities: The Souvenir in Native North American Art from the Northeast, 1700-1900*. Seattle & London: University of Washington Press, 1998.

Podedworny, Carol. "Mohawks in Beehives and Other Works," in *Parallélogramme* vol. 18, no. 2 (1992): 67.

Raheja, Michelle H. *Reservation Reelism: Redfacing, Visual Sovereignty, and Representations of Native Americans in Film*. Lincoln and London: University of Nebraska Press, 2010.

Rice, Ryan. *Counting Coup* [exhibition catalogue]. Santa Fe: Museum of Contemporary Native Arts, 2011.

Rice, Ryan. *Kwah I:ken Tsi: Oh So Iroquois* [exhibition catalogue]. Ottawa: The Ottawa Art Gallery, 2008.

Rushing III, W. Jackson, ed. *After the Storm. The Eiteljorg Fellowship for Native American Fine Art*, 2001. Indianapolis, Indiana: Eiteljorg Museum of American Indians and Western Art, 2001.

Ryan, Allan J. *The Trickster Shift: Humour and Irony in Contemporary Native Art*. Vancouver/Toronto: UBC Press; Seattle: University of Washington Press, 1999.

Ryan, Allan J. "I Enjoy Being a Mohawk Girl: The Cool and Comic Character of Shelley Niro's Photography," in *American Indian Art Magazine*, vol. 20, no. 1 (Winter 1994): 44-53.

Smith, Paul Chaat, "Home Alone," in *Reservation X: The Power of Place in Aboriginal Contemporary Art* [exhibition catalogue]. Hull, Quebec: Goose Lane Editions and Canadian Museum of Civilization, 1998.

Solomon, Beth and Cheryl Groch-Schriefer. *Hybrid Harvest: Contemporary Native American Arts* [exhibition catalogue]. Fullerton CA: California State University, 2005.

Sweet, Jill D. with Ian Berry. *Staging the Indian: The Politics of Representation* [exhibition catalogue]. Saratoga Springs NY: The Tang Teaching Museum and Art Gallery, 2002.

Taylor, Brandon. *Art Today*. London: Laurence King Publishing Ltd., 2005.

Townsend-Gault, Charlotte. "Kinds of Knowing," in D. Nemiroff, R. Houle, and C. Townsend-Gault, *Land Spirit Power: First Nations at the National Gallery of Canada* [exhibition catalogue]. Ottawa: National Gallery of Canada, 1992.

Varga, Darrell. "Seeing and Being in Media Culture: Shelley Niro's Honey Moccasin," in *CineAction*, vol. 61 (2003): 52-57.

Vigil, Jennifer, "Shelley Niro," in *St. James Guide to Native North American Artists*, ed. Roger Matuz. Detroit: St. James Press, 1998.

Wong, Lloyd. "Mohawks in Beehives," in *Fuse* vol. 16, no. 1 (1992): 38.

Other titles in the CAMS series:

Aganetha Dyck: The Power of the Small
by Julian Jason Haladyn

www.ingramcontent.com/pod-product-compliance
Lightning Source LLC
Chambersburg PA
CBHW020423220526
45464CB00002B/545